THE
HARMONY
OF NATURE
AND SPIRIT

BOOKS BY IRVING SINGER

Meaning in Life
1. The Creation of Value
2. The Pursuit of Love
3. The Harmony of Nature and Spirit

The Nature of Love
1. Plato to Luther
2. Courtly and Romantic
3. The Modern World

Mozart and Beethoven: The Concept of Love in Their Operas
The Goals of Human Sexuality
Santayana's Aesthetics
Essays in Literary Criticism by George Santayana (Editor)
The Nature and Pursuit of Love: The Philosophy
of Irving Singer (Edited by David Goicoechea)

THE
HARMONY
OF NATURE
AND SPIRIT

Volume Three of *Meaning in Life*

Irving Singer

THE JOHNS HOPKINS UNIVERSITY PRESS
BALTIMORE AND LONDON

© 1996 by Irving Singer
All rights reserved. Published 1996
Printed in the United States of America on acid-free paper
05 04 03 02 01 00 99 98 97 96   5 4 3 2 1

The Johns Hopkins University Press
2715 North Charles Street
Baltimore, Maryland 21218-4319
The Johns Hopkins Press Ltd., London

Library of Congress Cataloging-in-Publication Data will be found
at the end of this book.
A catalog record for this book is available from the British Library.
ISBN 0-8018-5426-1

To Roslyn,
For Her Generous Spirit

Contents

Preface

This book is a sequel to both *The Creation of Value* and *The Pursuit of Love*. The three constitute a trilogy, or triptych, about the good life. Though internally related to one another, they can be read in any order and independently of one another. Throughout *The Creation of Value* I distinguished between panoramic questions about a single, all-encompassing meaning of life that one might hope to discover and, on the other hand, meaningfulness that living entities are able to create for themselves in the natural world they inhabit. Most of the book dealt with the ways in which such meaningfulness comes into being and regardless of whether it eventuates in any commensurate form of happiness. In *The Pursuit of Love* I extended this approach by mapping the concept of love in relation to the human propensity to create meaning through a love of things, persons, or ideals and through self-love, sexual love, social love, and the varieties of religious love. Treating love as a search for meaning, I was able to bypass philosophies that try to reduce all love either to the physiological instinct of libidinal sexuality or else to a replication of what humankind receives from some theological source.

In the present book I use these earlier themes as leitmotifs in a further investigation not only of love, value, and meaning but also of their interaction with happiness that everyone wants and that many have considered paramount in the good life. I place this discussion in the context of traditional distinctions between nature and spirit that serve for me as a means of probing basic problems about whatever happiness or meaning is (or is not) available to us as human beings.

In the Introduction, I examine the concepts of nature and spirit and suggest that we can overcome the disharmony between them

only by recognizing spirit's place in nature itself. In Chapter 1
I discuss Schopenhauer's belief that true happiness is not possible
in the life of either nature or spirit, and in Chapters 2 and 3 I sketch
alternative ideas that avoid the negativism in Schopenhauer.
Presenting a view of nature that is less pessimistic than his, I argue
that the meaning we create in life gives us access to a kind of positive happiness he ignores. Instead of recommending a rejection of
nature, as Schopenhauer does, I consider in Chapters 4 and 5 the
possibility that we can get beyond the suffering in life either by
play, or by accepting our mere existence, or by consciously living in
accordance with nature.

These early chapters primarily seek to be exploratory; they
supply no comprehensive solutions to the relevant issues. Some
solutions begin to emerge from Chapters 6, 7, and 8, where I discuss imagination, idealization, art, and the aesthetic element of our
existence. I suggest that the harmonization between nature and
spirit, and between meaning, love, and happiness, arises from an art
of life that employs the same aesthetic principles as those that are
found in all artistic creativity. In Chapters 9 and 10 I apply this hy-
pothesis to valuation in general and to the phenomenology of ethics
and religion. In the last chapter I analyze love as a manifestation of
compassion, sympathy, and empathy, and show how the conclusions
in this book supplement those of the two that preceded it.

I do not think my reverberative mode of writing will be a
difficulty for most readers, but I know that some professional
philosophers may be puzzled by it. What exactly, they will say, is he
doing in this work? It does not belong to the dominant strands of
analytic philosophy or Continental postmodernist theory. It is not
ethics or aesthetics or even metaphysics as they are commonly
understood. How should this kind of discourse be classified? I
accept that as a legitimate question about all my recent books and
particularly about this one. I myself think of it as a type of *Weltbild*,
a world picture, as Wittgenstein would have said.

In his final manuscripts, Wittgenstein remarks that a world picture provides the framework and the fundamental grounding for all

other major beliefs that one might have but is not itself defensible by means of proofs or formal logic or even conclusive evidence. It is instead a general vision, and as such it cannot be established or refuted in the way that other theorization might be. Far from relying on consecutive argumentation, it communicates by means of what Wittgenstein calls "persuasion."[1]

In making this world picture, I have attempted to depict, as persuasively as I could, a philosophical naturalism that is meaningful to me in the sense of being foundational to everything I believe about human values, life, and nature as a whole. In many places the writing consists of speculative meditation rather than explicit delineation of steps that lead to a final inference. In this area of philosophy, intuitive insights are often more appropriate than syllogistic reasoning. I offer my reflections with no pretense of objectivity. Those who can profit from them may, however, feel encouraged to paint their own world pictures, naturalistic or not, similar to mine perhaps but ideally going beyond it in whatever manner expresses their own sense of being alive, their own need to *make* sense of what it is for anything to be alive.

❄

Among those whose comments and encouragement helped me to finish this book, I particularly want to thank W. Jackson Bate, Herbert Engelhardt, Felipe Guardiola, Eric Halpern, Marvin Kohl, Richard A. Macksey, Timothy J. Madigan, Arnold H. Modell, and W. V. Quine. I am also indebted to students in my MIT course "The Good Life" who criticized earlier drafts of the manuscript and to David M. Epstein as well as the other members of his faculty seminar on affect, in which one of its chapters was discussed. The book's contents served as the basis of public lectures I gave at several Spanish universities, in Madrid, Alcalá de Henares, Granada, Valladolid, Sevilla, Córdoba, and Málaga. I am grateful to the scholars who graciously made it possible for me to appear at these universities and above all to Cándido Pérez Gállego, Isabel Durán, José Antonio Gurpegui, Manuel Villar Raso, Juan J. Acero, José M.

Martín Morillas, José M. Ruiz Ruiz, Cayetano Estébanez, Francisco García Tortosa, Leocadio Martín Mingorance, Barbara Ozieblo Rajkowska, and their colleagues. Toward Willis G. Regier, who guided my book as one of his first projects as director of the Johns Hopkins University Press, I have a special feeling of gratitude.

I. S.

THE
HARMONY
OF NATURE
AND SPIRIT

❧

NATURE & SPIRIT

Throughout the history of philosophy one encounters distinctions between "nature" and "spirit" that seek to clarify an affective attitude many people have. It is a feeling that we, as human beings, belong to two worlds, two different realms of being. In the consciousness that is characteristic of our species there resides a sense that what pertains to us as natural entities is not identical with spiritual capabilities we also possess. We tend to think of our body as immersed in nature, and of our mind as a separate agency through which we transcend nature either literally or figuratively. Being a part of nature, we surmise that we belong to the flux of physical, quasi-instinctual forces that not only govern our organic needs but also prescribe the behavior appropriate for satisfying these needs. At the same time we readily assume that our human orientation toward values, ideals, and, in general, standards of good and bad indicates that we have a place in a spiritual dimension that exceeds the natural.

This way of distinguishing between nature and spirit is unacceptable to me. It precludes an adequate understanding of how consciousness, awareness, and the pursuit of ideal possibilities originate in nature, and it thwarts our attempt to find the conditions under which experience can be both meaningful and a source of happiness. To perceive how meaning in life may be united with the having of a truly happy life, and how the two may cooperate in the search for love, we need to discover the manner in which nature and spirit can interpenetrate within the dimensions of a good life suitable to our existence on earth.

Everything I will be saying issues from this "naturalist" point of view. In this chapter I lay the groundwork for my later analyses by examining some traditional approaches to the relationship between nature and spirit in the context of various ideas about religion, the religious attitude toward the world, spirituality of diverse sorts, and different paths of fulfillment that human beings have often followed.

I begin with a remark by the ancient Greek writer Archilochus. He said that the fox knows many little things but the hedgehog knows a single big one. In an article on Tolstoy that has become famous, Isaiah Berlin interpreted the character of empiricism, pluralism, naturalism, and nonreductivist belief in general as illustrating the fox's view of the world. In Tolstoy's impassioned quest for religious certitude he saw evidences of the hedgehog attitude. Berlin argued that Tolstoy was a fox who wanted to be a hedgehog: that was the key to his tortured soul.[1]

In this place I have little more to say about Tolstoy's fundamental problem. But Archilochus's distinction seems fruitful to me as a way of understanding the distinction between nature and spirit. In everyday existence we frequently feel a need to choose between two modes of living that we can pursue. One of them leads to greater complexity, the other to greater simplification. Each can provide its own kind of meaning, and both can ideally eventuate in a sense of happiness or well-being.

The first form of life consists in a willingness to accept multiple challenges that may appear at any moment. These challenges arise from our engagement with daily circumstances and are not always of great importance in themselves. On the contrary, the less important they are, the easier it is for them to become a source of happiness and even meaning. For instance, there is no deep significance in the fact that a leaky faucet allows a drop of water to escape every other minute. People who feel that they are inept in such matters, or too busy or too wealthy to bother about them, will simply hire a plumber (assuming they do not disregard the matter entirely). Such people do not allow the faucet to have anything more than a peripheral role in their life.

When faucets function properly, that is how we normally treat them. They become meaningful to us only when we pay attention to them, as we do if we focus on the drip and expend whatever energy or imagination is needed to eliminate it. Just to call the plumber is already a step in this direction, but repairing the faucet ourselves will obviously entail a greater personal involvement. We must diagnose the situation. Is it likely that a new washer will stop the drip? We must remove the old washer, if that seems indicated, and install another one of the same size. We must then reassemble the faucet, and so on. Particularly if the activity is new to us, we bestow importance upon it merely in carrying it out with some degree of diligence and efficiency. Whether or not we succeed in our plumbing venture, it helps to make our lives meaningful to an extent that is dependent upon the attention we bestow. If we enjoy this bit of practical behavior and if we are proud of what we have done, our effort may further in its limited fashion whatever happiness we are able to attain.

I have used an example that many will consider trivial, but I chose it precisely because it is so commonplace. The first of the two attitudes I mentioned cultivates challenges that present themselves in ordinary life, lack any cosmic importance or large-scale implications, and fit within our usual capacities. Gadgeteers but also technicians, scientists, and executives of every kind fill their lives with detailed efforts that are often comparable to changing a washer. In doing so, they experience meaning and occasional happiness that are unknown to people who disparage such interests or seek to liberate themselves totally from them. Though the fox may be a crass materialist whose system of values fills us with disgust, his ability to increase and to magnify the moments in which his life is both happy and meaningful for him may indeed seem enviable.

The second path can also provide meaning as well as happiness. It is the route taken by those who seek freedom from distractions that tie them to mundane existence and may be thought to constitute the sinfulness of temporality. Having the hedgehog's assurance that they know the single all-inclusive truth that explains reality as a whole, people of this sort feel that everything else becomes meaningful only in relation to it. And will this not yield the greatest happiness to anyone who can approach the demands of life with so great a truth in mind, not dealing with them as worthless impediments but rather as derivatives of the comprehensive revelation that applies to each necessity?

Men and women who seek the spiritual life have generally followed the second path. Whether they are ascetics who turn away from pleasures of the flesh, or mystics contemplating the One Which Is All, or metaphysicians probing their preferential access to ultimate Being, they search for meaning and happiness through a unified perspective that structures, sometimes even if that involves excluding, the "lesser" or "lower" interests engendered by our condition as natural entities. With its one big truth, the life of spirit may then seem to be inimical to the life of nature and its multiple but mainly vapid concerns.

In this book I explore the relationship between nature and the life of spirit, and, above all, the possibility that they can be harmonized with each other. Toward that end let me return, once again, to the fable of Aristophanes in Plato's *Symposium*. It is richer and even more suggestive than I, at least, had previously realized. Aristophanes himself offers it as an account of how love springs from our attempt to find the alter ego with whom we made a unity before the gods split us into isolated halves. Later in the dialogue Plato recasts the myth into his doctrine about humankind seeking oneness with the Good as the only object truly worthy of being loved. But if we remember that Plato believes the Good shows forth the nature of reality, we may go somewhat deeper in reinterpreting Aristophanes' fable. Not only is love a desire for unification with a valued object, and a principal effort to make life meaningful for ourselves, but also it seeks to overcome an ultimate division that pervades our very being.

As Aristophanes suggests, members of our species must always struggle with the fact that they are divided within themselves both collectively and individually. Philosophy, literature, and other arts have often tried to delineate the significance of this split. As a matter of scientific evidence, we may think it results from our evolution as creatures whose remarkable powers of consciousness and thought can function in partial separation from vegetative and appetitive faculties needed for survival. Though there be no mind without a body, our mind considers itself different from the body to which we know it is attached. Many related distinctions, both in ordinary language and in the history of ideas, reflect this primordial division that most of us take for granted.

Like other philosophers before me, I will be considering ways in which we can get beyond our sense of being split or divided in ourselves. In particular the concepts of nature and spirit have traditionally presupposed this type of alienation, each of them belonging to a system of ideas that fall into opposing classes. In one there are notions of time, mere becoming, matter, and organic drive that may culminate in happiness under favorable conditions. The other is constituted by concepts of eternity, the supernatural, being-in-itself, and a transcendental realm that reveals what is intrinsically valuable. How are we to make sense of these grandiose terms? Do the relevant ideas sustain the distinctions they articulate? And do these distinctions help us to understand what life is like, or to discern the elements of a life worth living?

In the past the two ideational clusters were often used to define alternate domains, distinct structures of ontology and of valuation. Everything we could accept as reality would then be envisaged as participating in one or another of these domains. And though becoming and being, or nature and the supernatural, or even happiness and the life of spirit, were treated as possibly interactive, they were defined as contrasting opposites. They were interpreted as having about them the type of clearly sketched outlines that we see in paintings by medieval artists like Giotto and Fra Angelico. The separation between this world and the "other" (higher) world was evident from the graphically depicted differences in coloration and composition within their works of art. As Pico della Mirandola later argued, human beings could have a life in either or both worlds. But the worlds themselves were conceived to be inherently detached from each other.

If this is our vision of reality, however, we need to explain how people can hope to have a good life in this world, how they can improve their lot on earth and attain whatever salvation is available to them. The traditional religions and philosophies offered one or another of two solutions to this problem. They imagined either an upward or a downward communication between the different realms, and sometimes simultaneous movement in both directions—as in the biblical image of angels traveling up and down on Jacob's ladder. Above all in the case of humankind, the upward direction involved the purification and possible sanctification of nature. Even if nature is what we are put here to rise above, as the Katharine Hepburn character says at one point in *The African Queen*, such elevation was usually thought to require a transformation of what is natural rather than its total annihilation. When this transformation occurs, the lower world emulates—and to some extent duplicates—the superlative qualities of the higher one. By seeking the Good, or following Christ, or cultivating standards of beauty, we would enable nature to penetrate (in one degree or another) the reality that lies beyond it. We might thereby experience heaven on earth. To that extent, the two realms are not considered wholly distinct.

For the most part, however, it was communication in the opposite direction that was given priority. Without an infusion of divinity, or some equivalent, it was thought that nature would not be able to rise above itself. Without God's foot on the pedal of the universe, nature could never achieve the energy needed for an upward movement. In more secular philosophies, such as Hegel's, Being was in principle more ultimate than Becoming but revealed itself throughout the varied manifestations of Becoming. As the English philosopher Bernard Bosanquet said, the real world is this one seen "concretely." In other words, we exist as part of a natural process, but we detect its meaning only by realizing that it shows forth an absolute reality—which is also an absolute ideality—that constantly transcends it. To acquire this splendid recognition, human beings had to develop a special talent that was sometimes identified as intuition and at other times as supreme rationality.

In my view all these philosophical systems are untenable. I believe that nature *is* our reality, that there is no other realm of being, that what counts for us as either knowledge or value must always derive from the fact that our life in nature consists of variegated responses idiosyncratic to ourselves. Those who thought that Being or divinity sanctifies nature by infusing it with sublime spirituality occasionally claimed that they too were naturalists in philosophy. In the doctrine known as pantheism, nature is identified with the deity, God and nature somehow being the same. Because Spinoza claimed as much, he was excommunicated on the grounds of atheism. But not infrequently in pantheism a distinction is also made between the aspect of nature that is God and the aspect that is not. In effect, this restores the original separation between the two ontological domains, even though they are portrayed as operating jointly within the empirical world. The naturalism I propose is more radical. It rejects entirely the original dualism.

At the same time I wish to avoid the reductivism that has vitiated the doctrines of earlier naturalists. They often repudiated concepts of ideal beauty, value, or spirit as either delusory or confused. In their eagerness to deflate metaphysical bigotry and tendentiousness, these naturalists became cynical scoffers. Since there is no higher realm to legitimize the ends and values that human beings espouse, and no sign of pure spirit in nature itself, they argued that ends or values or references to spirit are merely devices that people sometimes employ in their competitive struggle for mastery and survival.

This reductive type of naturalism makes the same kind of error that Descartes does in his formulation of skepticism. The idea of doubting everything may be justifiable, but the conclusion Descartes reaches—I think; therefore I am—is misleading. Descartes believes that he has attained a final stage of analysis in recognizing that since he is doing the thinking he at least must exist. What he does not see, or adequately appreciate, is that his ability to think implies the existence of other people and in fact the world itself. His experience as a thinker does not occur in a vacuum. It depends on language, beliefs, assumptions that originate and evolve in the human society to which he belongs. In having a specific content, his thinking addresses itself to a material universe that has existed for some time even though he, like all of us, is often deluded about it.

In a similar manner, those who wish to reduce the concepts of value and of spirit to ideas that seem less edifying or more scientific are often self-defeating. In their attempt to advocate an empiricism that will cleanse philosophical discourse of pomposity, they become incomplete and even truncated naturalists. Without our striving for ideals, without our faith in the importance of values that have always mattered to human beings, without our aspiration toward moral, aesthetic, and mainly spiritual achievements, we would not exist in nature as the species that we are. Nature is not inherently sacred or an embodiment of divinity, and yet these possible attainments are explicable in terms of natural phenomena that our imagination has singled out as worthy of acceptance. This kind of idealization is ingrained in our being, not merely as individuals but also as members of a primate strand that happens to have that innate predilection. The existence of this potential in human nature is undeniable. What needs to be investigated is the means by which it operates, how it employs the imagination, and how that can function in our lives as pervasively as it does.

In suggesting that idealization and imagination can help to explain our ways of talking about transcendence, Being, and spirit, I avail myself of the philosophical tools I found serviceable in my attempts to analyze the creation of value and the pursuit of love. Though the problems are significantly different in each case, they lend themselves to a similar mode of approach. We live in a world that in its totality seems to have no meaning to it, a world that exists in accordance with natural laws that are not themselves capable of expressing love or meaning or anything like them. Yet life itself, even among human beings who have become demoralized or have little or no sense of purpose, is always creating value and new forms of meaningfulness. These arise from within, as part of what it is to be alive, and in organisms such as ours they tend to issue into a need for love of one sort or another.

These facts of nature are most evident in creatures endowed with imagination that enables them to entertain varied possibilities beyond their actual existence from moment to moment. Our species has this capacity to an extraordinary degree, and that is why love and the quest for value-laden meaning matter so much to us. Through idealization our imagination fabricates and holds aloft goals that we consider exceptionally important. We bestow value upon them, as evidenced by our powerful affective responses as well as by the continual redirection of our behavior in conformity to these responses. We act this way because we are a part of nature and nature engenders such behavior in us. It is only in relation to nature as a whole that we can understand the nature of spirit. Far from being the revelation of eternity or some transcendental realm beyond the empirical world, spirit must be seen as a segment of nature that manifests its own unique employment of imagination and idealization.

For many people the mere conception of spirit issues from a sense of despair. They are convinced that the good life is not to be found here on earth. In feeling this, they are not just expressing disillusionment about the constitution of life on this meager planet. Their sentiments would not be altered if earth became more enjoyable or if they could travel to a galaxy that would provide greater opportunities for them to fulfill their heart's desire. To a great extent these men and women view the order of nature itself, and our immersion in it, with revulsion and disdain. They are like Dante's Francesca, who knows she is in hell because she succumbed to illicit sexual passion and yet laments that natural love can have this consequence. *E il modo ancor m'offende*, she tells Dante: "And the way of it still troubles me."[2] Those who long for another realm of being beyond the one that ordinary existence affords are often troubled that nature, even the nature of love, should be as it is. They tend to use words such as *spirit* to signify a type of reality that proves but also rectifies their dismal expectations about the world all human beings must experience from day to day.

Though I acknowledge the pervasiveness of this attitude, I want to find a different resolution for the problems from which it derives. For one thing, we must distinguish between spirit and spirituality, and we must recognize that both can be independent of what is normally deemed to be religion.

Rather than offering at the outset an explicit definition of spirit and the two other terms, I turn to a distinction that John Dewey made between "religion" and "the religious attitude." Dewey associated traditional religions with beliefs about a supernatural entity whose existence explains the being and condition of everything else. Dewey quotes a definition of religion that appears in the *Oxford Dictionary*: "Recognition on the part of man of some unseen higher power as having control of his destiny and as being entitled to obedience, reverence and worship."[3]

Like many others in the modern world, Dewey rejects the systems of belief that try to perpetuate past or present religions. He thinks they have been discredited by contemporary advances in science and philosophical analysis. But Dewey does not agree with those who infer that a *religious attitude* must therefore be avoided. He claims that there are "distinctively religious values inherent in natural experience."[4] He interprets the religious aspect of human life as a voluntary and enduring adjustment to our natural estate. This "adjustment" involves moral dedication that unifies the self without neglecting our subordinate role in the universe. "The essentially unreligious attitude is that which attributes human achievement and purpose to man in isolation from the world of physical nature and his fellows."[5] If we are religious, Dewey asserts, we recognize that our successes (both moral and physical) are contingent upon the cooperation of nature. In saying this, Dewey does not mean that piety involves submissiveness to natural occurrences. Neither does he limit the religious attitude to mere ecology. The religious extends beyond ethical involvement of a local sort. It broadens human vision to the universe at large as the final source from which ideals as well as individual realities come into being.

I mention Dewey's ideas, elusive as they may seem, in order to bolster our awareness that religion has no exclusive authority with respect to what is religious. Religion is compacted out of dogmas, theological theories, rituals, and institutional contrivances through which believers may share the company of those who have a faith that is similar to their own. None of this is required for the cultivation of a religious attitude. At the same time, I recognize that the community and the ideological paraphernalia ingredient in religion may serve a useful role for people who have need of them. Nor have I any reason to deny that many of those who belong to one or another religion succeed in developing an attitude we may consider religious. But the substantival noun specifies something different from the adjective, and it is important to see that what they individually refer to is not essentially the same. Religion and the religious are therefore independent of, though also compatible with, each other.

In saying this, I am disagreeing with Dewey's conclusions. He thought that religion and the religious are inevitably incompatible: "The opposition between religious values as I conceive them and religions is not to be bridged. Just because the release of these values is so important, their identification with the creeds and cults of religions must be dissolved."[6] On my view, one need not make this kind of dissolution—at least, not a priori or as universally requisite for all people under all conditions. One need only say that every religion must justify itself on its own, but without our foreclosing in advance the possibility that each may be justifiable. Religion can no longer promote its dogmas by claiming that it alone engenders religious values. This much of what Dewey says seems to me correct. Beyond that, however, every person must decide for him- or herself whether a specific religion helps or hinders the achievement of a religious attitude.

But what exactly is involved in this religious mode of living? My ideas about spirit and spirituality may provide some clues once we have clarified both and seen their differing roles in the life of human beings. Life and spirit are not the same. Life has many properties unrelated to spirit. Much of life consists of mechanisms that are, or seem to be, wholly routine, even preprogrammed. To a large extent we are what we are by virtue of habitual responses that have developed in us. Since mind and body, consciousness and materiality, are not totally distinct from each other, organisms such as ours can never be pure spirits. They nevertheless experience themselves as spirits, and they readily observe the presence of spirit in creatures like themselves.

Spirit consists in the self-oriented capacity of living beings to change the world in accordance with their own aspirations. In addition to being a biological phenomenon that follows rigid patterns and predictable means of survival, life is—to whatever degree and often haphazardly—creative throughout its spectrum. Spirit is the consecutive energy or thrust that appears as a family resemblance within the different ways by which living entities manipulate their surroundings.

If there were nothing involved but manipulation, spirit would merely be an aggressive desire to impose one's will. But though it cannot exist without volition, spirit is that much of life which directs the will toward novelty and innovation in the service of something consciously considered good. This last clause is crucial. Many organisms are motivated by an impulse to rearrange existence for the sake of getting what seems to be good for themselves. But the idea of goodness is too abstract for most creatures to imagine it in itself or as a concept. Spirit is needed for that. In being highly evolved both cognitively and affectively, spirit may even activate ideas about underlying goodness, value uniquely objective and authentic. That is why theorists have often claimed that spirit can fully occur only in human beings, or else in gods who resemble human beings in having conceptualization of this sort. Nevertheless, spirit remains a natural potency, subject to the laws of nature, that differs from volition in being directed toward goods that normally exceed our own immediate interests or desires.

The notion of spirit, and particularly what is called "the human spirit," contains a suggestion of momentum and progressivity built into it. We think of the human spirit as something that links person to person and augments from generation to generation. Hegel saw it as the highest reach at any moment of an absolute spirit that unfolds dynamically through all of time. His idea is true to the buoyancy we associate with the human spirit. Life keeps bounding forward as if reaching for ever more rewarding goals. If we study the actual data, however, we have little reason to think that spirit is forever making progress. Life always flutters on, but its destiny is never assured. Life transforms itself creatively, and in *Homo sapiens* it changes vastly as it evolves across the years. But even in humankind at its best, spirit is not invariably progressive.

Still, the very fact that the human spirit treats progress as a possibility native to itself tells us something of importance. Spirit as it exists in human beings yearns for self-improvement. This longing results from our having the ability to conceive of infinite goodness for which we hunger. The fabrication of, and subsequent striving toward, remote ideals is typically human. Perfectionism that renders us dissatisfied with our current capabilities, thereby instigating endless search for meaningful accomplishments, sets our species apart from all others. The human spirit is constantly engaged in both seeking and creating values, whether or not it advances uniformly.

Though ordinary people often speak proudly of the human spirit, the men and women who further it most may not be aware of how much they do so. The concept of spirit is either too philosophical or too amorphous for it to be clearly present in the mentality of many persons who live creative lives. Great painters may feel a force within themselves that enables them to make works of art whenever it erupts and allows itself to be harnessed by their technique. They may even think of it as an inspirational power that uses them to be its funnel or transmitter. But if we ask them more specifically what they do in their productions, they may only reply that they are experimenting with pigments on a canvas, or playing with different ways of organizing forms and materials, or simply tapping a gamut of possibilities in the visual arts. They may never say that they reveal the human spirit struggling in its perfectionism to attain an ideal goodness through acts that creatively reconstitute nature.

That kind of characterization is typically philosophical; it arises in the mind of a philosopher, and usually not in the thinking of an artist. All the same it can be an accurate indication of what the artist experiences while focusing on technical problems. His or her success in solving these problems may be apparent only to an appreciative student of the relevant art form, but it can also be seen as a triumph for the human spirit.

✳

Thus far I have avoided the word *spiritual*. Although this is the adjective that pertains to *spirit*, it is both vague and ambiguous. As they may shrink at the idea that they are the bearers of the human spirit, so too may artists who convey it shy away from any suggestion that they themselves are spiritual. They love the paints they apply or the clay their fingers mold, and possibly their models as well. They do not wish to clutter their mind with pretentious abstrusities, though on occasion they may talk about their artistic ideals in language that others find wildly mystical. If we say that someone is spiritual, we tend to think of that person as a sensitive plant, an ethereal being that has liberated itself from earth-bound materiality. The artist may be nothing of the sort. More to the point, however, spirituality differs from spirit in having a particular life of its own. Spirit is an aspect of life in general, but the *spiritual life* is a special way of living, and therefore it incorporates spirit in a manner that differs from other attempts to make life meaningful.

To illustrate the concept of spirit, I described the behavior of creative artists. I will do the same later with spirituality, but initially at least we are more inclined to cite the lives of the saints. Since spirituality involves a uniquely imaginative use of spirit, saints may also be considered creative and even practitioners of an art. But the self-expression they cultivate has often been the expressing of a self that seeks its own abnegation. That is spirituality of a negative sort, an optional form that ascetics and other extremists choose in their eagerness to avail themselves of anything that can induce self-purification. Such behavior may catch the ecclesiastic fancy and possibly cause these persons to be revered. But men and women who are more wholesome in their saintliness have no need of histrionics. Their conduct is directed toward selflessness that does not degenerate into a desire to hasten their own destruction. The saints most worthy of adoration understand full well that they will be annihilated in due time, like all other living entities, but they see no necessity to dramatize this looming fate. Their spirituality consists merely in their willed subjugation of their own willfulness, in their assertive acts of beneficial submissiveness, in their staunch though reluctant ability to accept suffering in themselves for the sake of alleviating it in others.

In pursuing the spiritual life through responses of this kind, the saintly attitude may well seem to be paradoxical. The saints are themselves usually dissatisfied with their actual level of spirituality. They are not serene, like Chinese sages or Stoic philosophers pleased with their noble detachment. The saints are troubled. They are aware of how much willfulness still remains in them, and of how much more one must do in order to diminish the overall suffering in the world.

The paradoxes to which I refer reveal the impossibility of denying oneself while also wanting to be efficacious as a self that prevails in its attempts to help others. But the healthy-minded saints accept their anomalous state and do what they can. Their efforts are worthy of our admiration, even if they are basically incoherent. We may disregard the dreary philosophy that some of the saints rely on in their desire to justify the spirituality they seek. We may even feel that their doctrinal utterances generally evince intellectual weakness rather than superhuman insight. And we may believe that most of them, devoted to worthy ends as they may be, have not managed to improve life on earth very much. If we continue to stand in awe of their proud struggle with materiality, we do so because we recognize that they are thereby bestowing value upon spirit as a threatened principle in life, and that this is what they really worship.

Since spirituality is the concerted effort to preserve, through acts as well as ideas and feelings, the creative force that is spirit, one can well understand why spirituality has traditionally been taken to represent the religious attitude. Established religions have been able to arrogate that honorific term to themselves because they learned, early on in the history of our species, how to integrate spirituality with the legends and the rituals that people can easily digest. But just as adherence to a religion is not the same as being religious, so too is spirituality no assurance that being named a saint means having an authentic religious attitude. In his distrust of the human ability to attain true saintliness, Luther suggested that an impulse in that direction comes from the devil and not from God. Even if Luther was right, however, he failed to recognize that most of the official saints whose sanctification he rejected also had doubts about their attempts to overcome what they called sinfulness in themselves. We need not sit in judgment on this issue. We need only conclude that the religious attitude is not necessarily present in spirituality approved by a particular religion and may well occur in the absence of it.

Indeed, the spirituality that most religions advocate has very often been negative. It then encourages attitudes of renunciation and unremitting hostility toward our natural condition. It defines itself as the repudiation of nature rather than the consecration of it. Instead of being an expression of spirit that is vibrant in its creativity and imagination, spirituality in this phase is sicklied o'er with the assurance that life consists of misery more than happiness, suffering more than joy, decline more than growth. When spirituality is healthy or benign, it is not like that: it is then affirmative, not negative. It glories in whatever goodness and beauty there is in nature, and it seeks to increase them.

Throughout this book I will be searching for the spirituality that contributes to our self-realization as natural beings, rather than any self-renunciation. Here I can only remind you that we often use religious language in contexts that are quite remote from either traditional religion or negative spirituality. We talk about men and women who are "saintly" in their devotion to their discipline or profession. We think of Socrates and Spinoza as persons who lived saintly lives. Their "religion," so to speak, was primarily the love of truth, and their dedication to the doing of philosophy was so intense that they were willing to sacrifice their comfort and security to this life-enhancing activity.

The same could be said about many artists who are driven by a sense of their aesthetic mission. Scientists may sacrifice all else in life to the pursuit of the knowledge that only they can provide. This heroic commitment within oneself is surely a kind of spirituality, and the metaphoric ascription of a religion may also be acceptable. Such extraordinary individuals show forth the religious attitude, and they do so without having to believe in dogmas of self-denial ordained by supernatural fiat.

Though most religions encourage dogmatic thinking of that sort, neither the religious attitude nor positive spirituality does. The life of spirit sets up no conceptual barriers that prevent one from enjoying any or all of the goods that nature offers. Spirituality that is negative and self-despising rejects the nature that sustains it even in its act of rejection. It therefore tends toward puritanism, which George Santayana describes in one place as "a natural reaction against nature."[7] Since the spiritual life need not be puritanical, however, its devotion and its dedication can be supremely consummatory, a fulfillment rather than a dying away. It then appears as a religious attitude that formal religions have attacked all too frequently—an attitude that dares to be joyful as well as meaningful, gratifying as well as humane, self-assertive as well as compassionate, and wholly naturalistic in its theoretical assumptions.

SCHOPENHAUER'S PENDULUM: IS HAPPINESS POSSIBLE?

When human beings experience pleasure, contentment, joy, or what they consider happiness, they usually feel that all's well with the world. Their experience may even assure them that they are in touch with reality. They easily conclude that they have found the meaning of life, that it shows itself in the mere fact that they are happy. As Wittgenstein said, "the man who is happy is fulfilling the purpose of existence."[1] That, at least, is what one feels in moments of happiness.

Optimists in philosophy have lent cognitive support for this feeling. The optimistic attitude has guided democratic and humanistic thinking for the last two or three hundred years. Happiness is taken to be not only an experiential good that all men and women can attain in principle but also one that makes their lives meaningful. A wise and moral society would therefore tend to maximize it whenever possible.

It is this belief that philosophical pessimism seeks to refute. The greatest of all pessimists in philosophy was Arthur Schopenhauer. Though his arguments have generally been neglected by English and American philosophers, they are now receiving new attention. In trying to prove that the world is not beneficently designed or ultimately concerned about the fulfillment of human interests,

Schopenhauer claimed that happiness is a rare phenomenon and, when it does occur, "negative" rather than positive. He meant that happiness is always relative to some prior evil that people are struggling to escape. Happiness is never a pure achievement. Our ability to experience it is tainted by the presence of an unwanted and undesirable element in our being: namely, our condition as creatures that undergo want or desire itself. For us to be happy, there must have been something we did not have, something we lacked and now must labor to obtain. The situation is inherently negative, Schopenhauer thinks, because the wanting of anything bespeaks deprivation, and that is already a type of suffering. As a prerequisite for life in general, this condition cannot be changed by any experience of happiness. Those who think we were "made" to be happy are fooling themselves.

If happiness were a positive and fundamental part of our existence, Schopenhauer says, it would occur spontaneously, pervasively, and without being dependent on the misery that comes from not having whatever it is we lack and therefore seek. Since happiness must be preceded by the undesired wanting of what we do not have, followed by a stressful striving to get it, the outcome must always be uncertain and often fruitless. Even when our effort makes progress toward its goal, it is still a discontent, since it forces the organism to act in ways that are not themselves intrinsically valuable. Living creatures want what they want, but usually they do not want the wanting or the pursuing of it. As a result, gratification—assuming it eventuates—can only exist within a context of basic unhappiness.

Moreover, Schopenhauer insists, the getting of what one wants is not a guarantee of prolonged satisfaction. Though the reaching of our goal may make us happy for a while, the gain does not last. By quieting the original desire, our success creates satiety. But that quickly turns into boredom, which is a form of unhappiness. The constant that defines human experience is thus suffering in one modality or another. To the extent that the search for happiness liberates us from an evil, it merely leads to later evils that result from our having coped with the earlier one.

Schopenhauer formulates his conception through the following image of a pendulum:

> The basis of all willing . . . is need, lack, and hence pain, and by its very nature and origin [the organism] is therefore destined to pain. If, on the other hand, it lacks objects of willing, because it is at once deprived of them . . . by too easy a satisfaction, a fearful emptiness and boredom come over it; in other words, its being and its existence itself become an intolerable burden for it. Hence its life swings like a pendulum to and fro between pain and boredom, and these two are in fact its ultimate constituents. This has been expressed very quaintly by saying that, after man had placed all pains and torments in hell, there was nothing left for heaven but boredom.[2]

The word *pain* that this translation uses, as most others do, is a suitable equivalent for Schopenhauer's original. But the German terms that he employs, notably *Schmerz* and *Leiden*, should not be taken to mean pain that is essentially physical. Critics who have misconstrued his terminology in this manner have sometimes remarked that desire does not always signify an attempt to eliminate physical pain. As one of them says: "Someone who desires to go for a walk or read a certain book will not be affected by painful sensations if his desires remain unfulfilled."[3] As a generalization this is quite true, but it misses the point. The painfulness of the human dispensation to which Schopenhauer refers is the sorrow or distress that exists in being unfulfilled, in not having what one desires before or even after one tries to get it. The suffering he considers fundamental is mental and metaphysical whether or not it is also felt as a localized sensation. It is a hardship in life itself, since everything that lives wants something or other it does not have, or else the continued possession of what it does have but must always fear it may lose.

Even in this formulation, however, Schopenhauer's message has been unpalatable to most of his readers. Is this because, as he would say, our desperate yearning for happiness deludes us all, philosophers as well as nonphilosophers? Or is it possible that something in the nature of living entities, including human beings, defeats

Schopenhauer's pessimistic conclusions? But, in this less than paradise that we inhabit, what could that be?

One of the telling arguments against Schopenhauer's pessimism that has been suggested runs as follows: Schopenhauer analyzes human experience in terms of two contrasting phases or conditions, the wanting of something one does not have and the eventual attaining of it; he assigns happiness to the experience of attainment but claims this consummation does not last; what he neglects is the fact that striving for the desired object can provide happiness in itself, happiness that endures as long as one enjoys the purposive pursuit and feels that progress is being made. In other words, happiness does not come from the mere elimination of want or deprivation. It also, and more characteristically, issues out of instrumental activities that yield prior satisfactions on their own.

This kind of argument appears in the writings of various nineteenth-century Romantics who maintain that happiness results from the act of searching for happiness, as opposed to the attaining of a previously desired object or goal. But would it not follow from this that the search for happiness is therefore illusory? We want and seek particular goods because we think they will make us happy. If, however, it is only the act of wanting and seeking that causes happiness, are we not invariably deluded about the so-called goods we wished to have? Having got them, we can no longer care about them; in fact, we must immediately reject them, since happiness, as we learn, is produced by pursuit alone. The problem is expressed in lines of a song by Irving Berlin (sung with ambivalent suggestiveness by Marilyn Monroe): "After you get what you want/You don't want it!"

Of course, many Romantics, Stendhal for instance, were not deterred by the possibility that happiness is based on illusion. That, they believed, is just the price one must pay to be happy. Since happiness consists in striving itself, they were willing to accept whatever self-deceptions enable us to strive at all.

In his book *Schopenhauer and Nietzsche*, Georg Simmel articulates a sophisticated version of the Romantic belief that happiness belongs to search and not attainment. He argues that Schopenhauer ignores the way in which "the hope for happiness turns into the happiness of hope."[4] According to Simmel, lasting gratifications, in love for instance, "come through an uninterrupted increase, not in a big leap from pure misery to pure happiness."[5] Simmel concludes that real happiness "is merely an accompaniment of strife, quest, and endeavor, such that achievement of the goal does not only fail to provide added happiness but is as irrelevant as is a beacon after one has put into port."[6]

This way of criticizing Schopenhauer is valid in one important respect. It calls attention to the fact that happiness is a state that depends on one's general attitude toward life rather than being geared to the getting of something one desired which may or may not satisfy. The person who lives in hope or feels that he or she is making progress toward some cherished goal can experience authentic happiness throughout the requisite pursuit. Whatever happiness results from getting what one wants is an incidental supplement to the pervasive goodness in having this affirmative attitude. To the extent that Schopenhauer ignores such realities, his pessimism deserves to be attacked.

All the same, Schopenhauer's critics have failed to recognize the subtlety of his thinking. For he perceives, more clearly than they do, the possible confusion or absurdity that always lurks within the happiness of searching for happiness. He sees the peril in hopefulness that makes us happy before we attain whatever object we are seeking. To enjoy the process of pursuit, we must believe that it will have an outcome we desire, and also that each stage in our endeavor belongs to a pattern that is meaningful by virtue of that desired outcome. But if the world, in human experience and in the universe at large, is as Schopenhauer portrays it, all enjoyment is more or less ephemeral as well as uncertain. Our feeling of anticipatory happiness reduces to wish fulfillment that propels us forward but scarcely alters the underlying suffering to which we are doomed.

If that condition is indeed unavoidable, Schopenhauer's overall pessimism would seem to remain unscathed.

In arguing that the fundamental structure of our experience is thus determined by the alternation between lack and boredom, Schopenhauer does not deny that there may be ways in which one can learn how to deal with this state of affairs. In effect, he sketches two tactics available to persons who have become enlightened through his philosophy. The first of these tactics is only melioristic, but the second introduces a path of salvation that Schopenhauer staunchly advocates. The lesser remedy involves stoical acceptance of the fact that happiness can never be more than superficial, given what life is like. Once we know that suffering is universal and inescapable, we will be better prepared to face the ills that attend misfortune or old age. We will recognize the inevitability of such sorrows, and we may even be comforted by the reflection that "our present suffering fills a place which without it would be at once occupied by some other suffering which the one now present excludes."[7] Schopenhauer does not deny that some sufferings can be worse than others, but he thinks that believing all of life is normally suffering in one form or another conduces to a sense of relative peace. He doubts, however, that many people will ever have the rationality needed for this salutary outlook.

Describing the second tactic, Schopenhauer notes that the greatest misery in human existence occurs when the pendulum swings back and forth too violently, or else remains too long arrested at either of the termini. The greater our deprivation, in quantity or length of time, the greater our suffering; and the same is true about the boredom that follows upon the elimination of the original lack. We lessen the unhappiness of life by reducing the gap between the alternatives. All satisfaction of desires can lead to boredom, but if our consummatory experience is quickly succeeded by new desires, boredom will have little scope and scant duration. Similarly, the needs and organic drives that motivate our ongoing

search for happiness will not be experienced as a devastating suffering if they occur within a process that includes gratifications that
both precede and follow them.

In his delineation of this alternative, Schopenhauer says that
causing "desire and satisfaction to follow each other at not too short
and not too long intervals, reduces the suffering occasioned by both
to the smallest amount, and constitutes the happiest life."[8] But
Schopenhauer is not sanguine about the attainability of this level of
happiness. In only manipulating the movement of the pendulum, he
says, we do not liberate ourselves from the suffering and depen-
dency built into our condition. Even when we have experience that
controls the elements of striving and satiety, our life is still governed
by a succession of unwelcome lacks and ineluctable feelings of
boredom. In order to minimize the intervals between desire and
satisfaction, Schopenhauer claims that we must cultivate methods
of withdrawing, as completely as possible, from all conceivable fluc-
tuations of the pendulum. He insists that the "purest joy . . . lifts us
out of real existence and transforms us into disinterested spectators
of it." This derives from "pure knowledge which remains foreign
to all willing, [from] pleasure in the beautiful, [and from] genuine
delight in art."[9]

These are the directions in which Schopenhauer later explores
the spiritual paths that afford whatever salvation is available to
humanity. But they scarcely alter the extent of his pervasive pessimism. For he insists that very few people can follow these paths of
salvation. And even those fortunate persons who are able to must
undergo a kind of suffering that others do not experience. The
higher one flies, Schopenhauer says, the more lonely one becomes
and the more prone to difficulties caused by one's rare and elevated
efforts.

Schopenhauer tries to support his metaphysical insights with
evidence about human nature. On the one hand, he states, we
observe that human beings do not feel lesser sufferings when they
are being tormented by greater ones, but once a major source of
suffering has been eradicated minor discomforts take on more importance and occasion more unhappiness than they would have

formerly. It is as if suffering is our permanent lot: if we avoid it in some fortunate situation, we will undergo and magnify its effect elsewhere in our life.

On the other hand, Schopenhauer insists, even a happiness that we have sought and long anticipated will not create a lasting change in our condition. Though we may greet some achievement with delight, the sense of joyfulness does not endure. We fear that our serendipity will disappear, and sure enough, it soon turns into either boredom or a restless search for some other experience that will also yield only a brief escape from the wretchedness of wanting something. This is not what people expect when they are carried away by hopes of happiness, but Schopenhauer believes it is what always occurs. He concludes that, common as it may be, the search for happiness is founded on fallacies that only philosophical pessimism can explain and possibly dispatch.

Schopenhauer's approach stands in opposition to the lifestyle of those in the modern world who seek for little more than happiness. If Schopenhauer is right, this attitude is both delusory and unavailing. If positive happiness cannot be obtained, deprivation and suffering being fundamental in all of life, no satisfactions will ever provide a viable solution for the problems of humanity. But possibly these two perspectives, contradictory as they may initially seem to be, are really inwardly united as facets of a single viewpoint that they jointly share. Proust suggests in one place that the *quoiques* (the althoughs) of life are really the *parce ques* (the becauses). The puzzlement of Monsieur Norpois being extremely good about answering correspondence and attending to the needs of his friends although he is a very busy statesman dissolves once Marcel realizes that it is *because* Norpois is so busy that he organizes his official duties in a way that enables him to be conscientious in his private life.[10]

Similarly, it may be the case that people who devote themselves to the ever-present hope of happiness are really manifesting presuppositions not entirely different from Schopenhauer's. Although they would seem to believe that happiness is a positive good and a

perennial resource for human beings, it may be that they give themselves to every momentary possibility of its occurrence because they
secretly despair of finding any circumstance in which it can truly survive. Their behavior indicates that basically they are as pessimistic
as Schopenhauer is. He would argue that they live in illusion and
therefore demonstrate the validity of his general vision.

Schopenhauer's philosophy may take on further interest if we
compare it to the myth of Sisyphus. As a symbolic portrayal of the
human predicament, that myth has been employed by Camus and
others on the peripheries of twentieth-century existentialism who
might have been expected to feel revolted by Schopenhauerian
metaphysics. Nevertheless, the image of the pendulum can serve
as a theoretic model that explains the myth Camus analyzes. We
may interpret the punishment inflicted on Sisyphus not only as his
having to push boulders laboriously up a mountain but also as his
feeling hope each time he begins the task to which he has been condemned. At the beginning of his difficult project, he anticipates an
imminent happiness that will reward his efforts once he has reached
the top; and possibly, at the summit, he may experience a momentary feeling of joy. But it only serves as a cruel mockery, for real
happiness will never occur. Even if the boulder lingers before de-
scending, it soon topples. Whatever satisfaction Sisyphus may have
had changes into a sense of total desperation. Unless we can free
ourselves of Schopenhauer's type of pessimism, we cannot escape
this depressing implication in the myth. Both accounts contribute
to the notion that life in nature, ordinary existence as it is usually
lived, is pointless.

In attempting to go beyond these varieties of pessimism, we
must recognize that each expresses profound indignation at the
idea that suffering should even exist. This would seem to be what
Schopenhauer feels most strongly. In him, and in Camus as well, I
think, there lurks the feeling that no occurrences of happiness can
outweigh or discount the enormous suffering that life involves.
Though Schopenhauer grieves because the quantity of misery in
the world is always greater than the happiness in it at any time, that
is just a secondary consideration for him. He is horrified not only

by the amount of suffering he perceives but also by the fact that it is mostly unredeemable: it comes into being within a vital matrix that may never lead to happiness and generally does not. Cold and scornful as he may seem to be, Schopenhauer is tormented by the mere phenomenon of suffering. He depicts it as a tragic blight that permeates all of nature, a universal blemish that remains constant and inescapable throughout life in its totality.

If we ignore this intuition and its corollaries, we will not be able to appreciate the great importance of Schopenhauer's thinking. When we consider that life feeds cannibalistically on itself, and that every creature about to be devoured by another resists the destruction to which it must submit, we recoil from the hideous spectacle. Schopenhauer rubs our nose in it and forces us to draw the dire conclusions we would so eagerly avoid.

In our heart of hearts, we all want Schopenhauer to be wrong. Like Simmel and the traditional optimists who are dismayed by Schopenhauer's philosophy, we want to chip away at the premises in his argument. I believe this can be done with a certain degree of success. But here, as elsewhere, it may be profitable to assume a worst-case scenario. What follows if we agree with Schopenhauer that suffering is more fundamental in our natural and ontological state than whatever happiness we can achieve either by attaining some desired goal or by seeking it with hopefulness? Schopenhauer does not wish to induce feelings of utter failure. He rejects the idea that suicide can be a solution to life's problems. He thinks that acceptance of his doctrine will free us from dogmatic stupidities and enable us to work out our salvation with diligence, as the Buddha said, but also with intelligence, good will, and genuine knowledge about our own reality. In order for us to acquire this commendable attitude, Schopenhauer insists that we must first repudiate the life force itself, which he calls collectively "the will" and which he associates with our wanting anything we do want.

At this point, I suggest, Schopenhauer misconstrues the human import of his pessimistic premises. Even if we agree that our experience fluctuates between extremes of lack and boredom, what does that entail? Not a belief that happiness is impossible, or even secondary to overall suffering, but rather that the terminal reaches of the pendulum define conditions that we must always ward off. There is no reason to assume that only a handful of exceptional individuals can manage to control the swinging of the pendulum, or that success in this endeavor requires withdrawal from ordinary life and a complete negating of the will.

Schopenhauer's basic error consists in his neglecting the actual dynamics of a life that can be happy or gratifying. In treating ennui as the likely outcome of obtaining a desired goal, he does not see that a living organism is programmed to use both the accomplishment and the boredom to which it may lead as a springboard for further satisfactions in the future. Only in extreme cases of psychological disability, or when success comes too easily and is meaningless, do we become arrested in our previous consummations and thereby trapped within a deadening sense of boredom. What commonly occurs, and in no way depends on the "pure knowledge" that Schopenhauer recommends, is an adaptive process within each organism which enables it to develop in ways that are often unforeseeable. After some momentous achievement there may be a period of exhilaration or repose, followed perhaps by boredom, but these serve as a prelude to later activities. Normally there is not even a final termination of the original quest, since the contents of our previous experience are recycled as a resource for subsequent desire and exploration. Our happiness resides in this continuous process.

Schopenhauer's analysis is mechanistic: it fails to appreciate the vital flux that links each moment of gratifying achievement with ongoing and expansive developments. Unless boredom persists as a sheer malfunction in the flow of life, it makes an essential contribution to the search for additional satisfaction. This is not inevitable, of course, but neither is Schopenhauer justified in assuming that getting what we want must always issue into prolonged and debilitating sorrow.

Following Schopenhauer's inspiration, Oscar Wilde said that the two tragedies in life are not getting what we want and getting it. The wittiness of this cynical remark turns upon the possibility that success of any sort may lead to overindulgence or disillusionment.

There is much truth in this, and the danger of failing *because* of our success is a peril that menaces all purposive behavior. But such failure is avoidable. It is extraneous to the immanent structure of vital desire and pursuit. It results from either a mistaken conception about the desirability of what we wanted, or else a distorted idea of the cost that is required in order to get it. These are great hazards that may beset appetitive experience. But we are able to surmount them more pervasively than Wilde or Schopenhauer thought. I return to this line of reasoning when I discuss in a later chapter John Dewey's ideas about "the continuum of ends and means."

At the other pole of his distinction, Schopenhauer provides an unconvincing portrait of desire itself. He may be right to think that wanting something is based on need or lack and that these signify a deprivation that can be classified as suffering. But this kind of suffering, which one may call "metaphysical," must not be confused with the suffering of a person who is ravaged by fever, starvation, or psychosis. Though these are frequent enough in animate existence, they are neither universal nor always irremediable. What is universal—our condition as beings that alternate between desire and satisfaction—is of a different sort. It often issues into creativity and stable growth, necessity serving as a benign, not hostile, mother of invention. Far from being horrified by our condition, we may see it as that which enables us to care about anything and to act constructively to make the world conform with whatever we do care about.

This kind of creativity can bring happiness as well as meaning, not only in our moments of accomplishment but also in our realization that having just the needs and lacks that we do have makes it possible for us to achieve our own fulfillment. If we repudiate that reality, if we are distraught at being creatures ontologically subject to deprivation in any form, we blind ourselves to the opportunities it regularly affords. That in turn generates a feeling of alienation from, and even hatred toward, the entire framework within which a living entity must operate.

When Schopenhauer expresses the negative sentiments in his philosophical analysis, and in his suggestions about paths of salvation, he is not responding throughout the totality of his being. He himself lives and breathes as a human organism. He has vegetative, sensory, kinesthetic, and emotional faculties through which he flourishes as a participant in life. But within the categories of his *thought*, he underestimates the positive importance of these faculties. His doctrinal pessimism is only a partial reaction promoted by his intellect. Through its powers of abstraction, the intellect separates us from the world insofar as it causes us to stand back, observe, and possibly reject what lies before us. The intellect is nevertheless an emanation out of nature, and it need not make itself into an opponent to what is natural. But in Schopenhauer's metaphysics, as in the response of many others, that has happened.

Refusing to accept the mere existence of deprivation, the very fact that needs and lacks occur at all, Schopenhauer turns against the life that flows within him and makes it possible for him even to have an intellect. And yet life sustains his rebellious cerebration willy-nilly, regardless of its treachery. Schopenhauer himself saw this as a paradox. He did not, however, realize the extent to which it undermines his entire philosophy.

As another way of formulating this criticism, we can say that Schopenhauer's approach indicates a lack of faith in nature. Throughout this book I try to clarify the possibility of "faith" in a context such as this, and how it serves the harmonization of nature and spirit. In the negative attitude that Schopenhauer evinces I detect a generalized distrust that should alert us to the shortcomings of his perspective. There is in Schopenhauer no appreciation of either the grandeur of nature or the goodness one might feel in knowing that one is a part of it. He rightly portrays nature's destructiveness, its ruthless causality, its willingness to disregard the ideals of humanity and in fact everything human beings value. That is why nature (the will) is for him so hideous and repellent. But he does not recognize the quasi-artful way in which the life force gets us to carry out its demands by *supporting* us in our being, as long as we manage to cooperate with it.

Through the mechanism of habit, nature guides us into responses we might not have tolerated otherwise. And when we enjoy our responses, whether or not they are habitual, savoring the vitality of their sheer appetitiveness, our actions and our desires seem appropriate, even prescribed in view of what life is like. The satisfactions that result renew our belief that we are at one with our surrounding environment. Once we have identified ourselves with material nature, it is easy for us to bestow value on it and even to see in it a purpose or good will not wholly different from our own. This primitive faith in nature is nature loving itself, much as the Christians said that God loves himself and that his love of what he has created is really a superlative form of self-love.

Faith of this sort issues from that "cunning of the will" that Schopenhauer understands so well in other aspects of his philosophy. It lies deep within human phenomenology and pervades our experience of the world, at least the world that we experience as our own. We may reject this kind of faith as debased submission to brute and meaningless laws of nature, and we may advocate resistance to it on many occasions, but we could not live without a residual acquiescence or suspension of antipathy. In his defiant romanticism, Schopenhauer asserts the dignity of the human soul that is always free to say no. His gesture may be admirable, but in the process of carrying it out he neglects the subterraneous compliance that nature has already instilled in him. Without such compliance he could not have fomented the ideas that enable him to disown nature.[11]

Though Camus understood the possibility of faith in nature better than Schopenhauer, his conception is also inadequate. As a solution to the problem of Sisyphus, Camus imagines the condemned man achieving a heroic posture that finally transcends his own punishment. Trudging down the mountain after pushing the boulder up in the usual way and watching it roll back as it always has, Sisyphus suddenly acquires the ability to accept this as his fate in life. Instead of reviling the gods or pitying himself, he now experiences pride in being what he is and doing what he must do. We may treat that kind of feeling as just another Romantic sentiment—in this case, euphoria rather than *Weltschmerz* or Byronic defiance—but it also bespeaks a faith in the order of things and in the fundamental being of nature. Boulders are such that they will naturally roll down a mountain. Sisyphus can accept this necessity,

and he can likewise accept the need that he or any other human being may have in wanting to push a boulder up a mountainside for
some particular purpose.

But can he truly acquiesce in the meaninglessness of doing what
the gods have visited upon him for all eternity? I find that hard to
believe. The redeeming faith toward which Camus is groping must
be defined in a different way. It must have relevance to what is truly
meaningful to human beings and not a wholly absurd (albeit joyful)
acceptance of meaningless existence.

To the degree that we consider life absurd, we cannot have the
faith in nature I have been trying to describe. Yet only as an expression of such faith is happiness possible for human beings. The requisite elements in this potentiality we must now explore.

2

BEYOND THE SUFFERING
IN LIFE

Insisting that all of life is based on deprivation and that even major gratifications cannot alter its characteristic suffering, Schopenhauer concluded that life is not worthwhile. The suffering in animate existence proved to him that the universe would be better without there being any life. One way of countering this argument is to claim that suffering, experienced as either pain or just discomfort, can help to make a life meaningful. In the idealist tradition of Western religion that Schopenhauer sought to discredit, this belief about the ultimate value of suffering was frequently asserted or assumed. Within a more secular perspective it enters into a short story by Chekhov, whose writing often reflects the influence of Schopenhauer's pessimism. In "Ward No. 6" Chekhov depicts the moral and psychological disintegration that a doctor in a mental ward undergoes once he begins to question the utility of his medical efforts. As a doctor, he must alleviate suffering whenever possible. But if his ministrations succeed, he argues, there may no longer be any need for religion or philosophy, and humanity would lose not only the happiness but also the meaning that these can offer. His reasoning ends as follows: "Pushkin underwent terrible torments before his death; poor Heine lay paralyzed for several years; why should an Andrei Yefimich or a Matrona Savshina be spared illness,

33

when their lives are null and would be utterly empty and like an amoeba's were it not for suffering?"[1]

We might say that the doctor's mode of thinking already indicates disorientation or mental illness on his part. But even so, we may wonder where his argument goes wrong. I believe his mistake consists in confusing cause and effect. The suffering that Pushkin or Heine felt did not bring their creativity into being, and the removal of suffering would not have necessarily made the lives of the two peasants either meaningless or insipid. The existence of suffering as an unwelcome reality in life does encourage people to find inventive means of comprehending and controlling it. Philosophy and religion play a role in this attempt, but so does therapeutic intervention. When medicine eradicates some particular suffering, it strengthens our desire to alter a world in which suffering is so common and lasting happiness so difficult to attain. In any event, Pushkin and Heine were great men not because of their suffering but because they were able to transmute their suffering into works of art that add to the meaningfulness of life.

But what if there were no suffering in the world? Though this question may seem fanciful, it will help us to understand the role that suffering plays in ordinary experience. Modern medicine, and many developments in recent technology, can be seen as part of a typically human struggle to eliminate suffering as much as possible. To the extent that humanity succeeds in this project, however, it modifies nature, and that is always risky. Interference with natural processes can result in collateral losses for one's own species as well as others. Changing the environment puts scenic beauty in jeopardy, and the ease or bodily comfort that may accrue can also do more harm than good.

Moralists throughout the ages have extolled the virtues of a strenuous life, as opposed to one that is carefree, on the assumption that the lot of humankind must always be to suffer in nature. Religious doctrines, to say nothing of the muscular activism that can issue from them, have often proclaimed that since suffering is basic to human nature the pursuit of pleasure or even happiness is inherently sinful. A more plausible view appears in the speculations of contemporary scientists such as the ethologist Konrad Lorenz. Like traditional sages of the East, Lorenz points out that our search for happiness and the avoidance of suffering can be dangerous when it succeeds too well. He remarks that every higher civilization discovers how quickly a life of pleasure and enjoyment deteriorates into vice and moral distress. He argues that the human ability to escape hardships and a difficult life is always problematic culturally. As advancing technology has made existence easier and more amenable to comfort, Lorenz remarks, "modern man has moved . . . in the direction of ever-increasing intolerance of all stimulus situations that produce unpleasurable experience and . . . [ever-increasing] apathy toward all pleasure-eliciting ones."[2]

Particularly in societies, such as ours in the West, that encourage consumption rather than parsimony, the need to escape unpleasurable experience at any cost diminishes the likelihood of people engaging in protracted efforts, even those that might have beneficial consequences. Lorenz claims that this explains our appetite for instant gratification, and he warns against the "entropy of feeling" to which the general syndrome leads. When people can satisfy their wishes without much difficulty, their pleasures are less meaningful and less valuable to them. Joy, as opposed to sensory pleasure, comes from achievements that have been wrested from the environment through focused and often persistent activity. Gratification based upon the avoidance of strenuous acts and stressful situations is likely to engender what Lorenz calls "deadly boredom."

In this conception of emotional entropy, we may see an advance upon the ideas of Schopenhauer. Lorenz is not suggesting that men and women are so constituted that their affective life must invariably swing between the extremes of deprivation and boredom. On the contrary, Lorenz believes that ennui occurs only when we automatically assume that all discomfort must be eschewed. Getting what we want is not the cause of boredom, but rather getting it without having struggled with the many obstacles that belong to the human condition. Far from being a pure negativity, suffering provides the opportunity to achieve well-being through the overcoming of these obstacles. They are not essentially calamitous, as

Schopenhauer thinks, but sometimes blessings in disguise—given the natural coordinates that define what it is for a human being to be blessed at all.

Lorenz recognizes how hard it may be to control the entropy of feeling in modern civilization. He thinks that just surmounting obstacles is not enough: they must be obstacles to our mere existence and vitality, in contrast to those that are artificially contrived. To some degree, Lorenz is surely mistaken in this belief. The joy of scoring a touchdown or climbing a mountain or bringing our income above some arbitrary number may be grounded in our human nature but is also relative to goals that we fabricate for the sake of proving we can reach them. In part, at least, our ideals are all contrivances of this sort. Though they issue out of nature, they project upon it aspirations we have created in order to make life more interesting and more meaningful. By instigating projects that give importance to chosen modes of struggling with the environment, we bolster our capacity to master and possibly enjoy realities that life has forced upon us. But the actual struggles are often highly artificial.

What I find most significant in Lorenz's account is his awareness of the programmed need to engage in meaningful activities regardless of how difficult they may be. He cites case histories of young people suffering from the boredom of emotional entropy who tried to commit suicide but bungled the attempt and only blinded or crippled themselves. He reports that they then lost all inclination toward suicide and eventually turned into "balanced, even happy people." He concludes that "a genuinely challenging obstacle with which they found themselves confronted made life again worth living."[3]

Many authors have pointed out that in time of war modern societies often manifest a decline in the number of people who suffer from depression and related mental illness. Faced with the immediacy of dealing with major difficulties, men and women can overcome the apathy and sense of pointlessness that result from pursuing one's own petty interests. In this situation, Schopenhauer might detect an additional illustration of the sorrow of being human. And he may be right, since the wars that cure our previous boredom lead on to greater devastation and misery. But war is not the only means of handling the problem. Having established the inadequacy of the pendulum metaphor, we may discover more effective ways to minimize suffering while also avoiding boredom.

❉

It would be disingenuous to suggest that our speculations can provide a definitive "solution" in these matters. Our predicament as human beings does not resemble a mathematical problem for which one can hope to find the right answer. In formulating ideas about a good and satisfying life, we may have to settle for assertions that are not provable and do not lend themselves to anything like objective certitude. A great deal depends on individual choices that we make and then must live with. Since it is always developing, the world of our experience depends, to a considerable extent, on decisions that require successive readjustments in our life. We may wish to fly long distances in an airplane, delighted to save the time and avoid the trouble of traveling on the ground. We may even like the idea of speeding over the countryside at an elevation that even birds cannot reach. But in the process we will have sacrificed the pleasures that come from observing fields, mountains, rivers, towns, cities at close hand, as a walker or bicyclist does. Similarly, every advance in technology nullifies various possibilities for enjoyment even though it makes life more comfortable or more exciting in some respect. The newly acquired benefits do not come without significant cost, particularly when we have to devote a great deal of time and energy to repairing or maintaining the artifacts of whatever technology has now become indispensable.

There are at least three ways of dealing with this problem. The first might be called the "Luddite" response. The Luddites were people in eighteenth-century England who tried to destroy early inventions of the industrial age on the grounds that they would dehumanize society and take away the jobs of many honest workmen. In the last two hundred years similar attitudes have occurred among persons who view with alarm the ever increasing growth of automation and robotics. The dehumanization that is most to be feared results from idleness itself. Even in societies that are wealthy enough to care for the physical needs of the entire population (through welfare payments or unemployment compensation), idleness has generally induced stultifying ennui. It is as if Schopenhauer's pendulum applies at a sociological level: those who do not work experience the boredom that comes from the technological successes designed to eliminate deprivations existing in preindustrial periods. The Luddite approach is based on the hope that society can solve this dilemma by going back to an earlier stage of economic development.

One might reply that "progress" cannot be reversed. But even if this is true in some panoramic sense, there do exist examples of technologies having been curtailed once they were found to be hazardous. Fewer nuclear plants are being built in the United States nowadays than were once anticipated, and the dangers they create may someday cause them to be inactivated completely. Still, that kind of case involves harm to the environment rather than the psychological perils of boredom resulting from unemployment. The Luddite approach addresses itself to the latter consideration.

The principal question in such issues is whether advanced technologies that seem to make it easy for people to get what they want are really thwarting their underlying search for happiness and general well-being. Though there may now be few societies that have not been touched by modern civilization, we should consider, if only as a parable, the issue that would be faced by members of some primitive tribe suddenly given access to present-day technology. Would they be better off joining the outside world and thereby gaining medicine, tools, and all the other appurtenances of a less arduous life than the one they are accustomed to? Or should they withdraw into the wilderness, where they will be immune from the debilitating lures of civilization as well as its inevitable annoyances?

In situations of this sort there is no answer that is universally right or wrong. Each group must decide its destiny for itself— assuming that the rest of humanity allows it to do so. Neither of the alternatives I have posed can wholly free us from the possibility of suffering. All that happens, either in furthering or impeding technology, is the choosing of one system of goods and evils rather than another. As there never was a golden age in which our species lived in blissful harmony with nature, so too will there never be a utopian state in which technology (or any other human development) will provide totally unalloyed happiness. A wise decision may improve the balance of goods and evils, but that must depend on the variables in each case.

The second of the three tactics I mentioned derives from renunciation of a sort that many religions have advocated. It is related to their conception of the world as a sinful place in which evil generally predominates over good. Whether the faith is Manichean or Buddhist or ascetic in the manner of various Christian sects, it holds that the root of suffering arises from the fact of desire itself. Eliminate the impulse to gratify our multiple needs, and the terrors of the pendulum will disappear. Eradicating or minimizing desires, we will not have to strive against an environment that has always been resistant to them. Since the getting of what we would have wanted yields only brief and fragile happiness, we will lose very little in having renounced the entire trajectory of pursuit and satisfaction. By no longer wanting anything, we will have armored ourselves against the pain of being frustrated as well as the boredom of having succeeded. Liberated from the enslavement to appetite, we may then cultivate the simplicity and serenity that reveal a stationary meaning in life. Perturbations of the spirit will have disappeared, and we can savor a type of earthly paradise.

This renunciatory attitude is unacceptable to most people, including myself, because it repudiates instincts that evolution has encased in our being and often with great profit to us. In turning away from all desire, asceticism calls for an annihilation of self. This, in fact, becomes one of its official doctrines, and it is justifiable as a reminder that much of what we associate with our "self" is really extraneous and unnecessary. At the same time, the ascetic approach is largely negativistic. It is a curling in despair rather than a vibrant or even viable solution. It confuses resignation, which is often essential in life, with renunciation, which never is. Having resigned ourselves to our condition as creatures whose desires are not always desirable, we can learn how to harness or restrain large numbers of them. To do this, however, is not to renounce desire as a whole, which may even be impossible.

In the ancient world the Stoics sought the path of renunciation, and their moral courage was sometimes exemplary. But the Epicureans had greater insight into the nature of human happiness. They strove for ways of living that would steer humankind away from useless distractions and alluring but ultimately dissatisfying pleasures. The Epicureans were resigned to the fact that people have limited capacities for enjoyment. They recognized that a truly successful life renounces no desires a priori but tolerates only those that lead to fulfillment and actual goodness.

The third avenue of approach, the one that means most to me, is a variation upon the Epicurean attitude. It is not enough just to devote oneself to the amassing of pleasures. Even to think in these terms suggests an intellectualized, and therefore distorted, mode of behavior. The philosophical belief in hedonism, to which most Epicureans have traditionally subscribed, is open to criticism that may seem obvious nowadays. Opponents of this view have often pointed out that happiness is not increased, and may often be diminished, by a single-minded dedication to pleasure as such. One might even argue that people could not enjoy doing what they pleasurably do if they cared only about the having of pleasures. The pleasure of working in the garden does not come from seeking just the *pleasure* of working in the garden. One has to like gardening, and the effort it entails. The search for pleasure is one thing; the undertaking of activities we enjoy because they matter to us is quite different. The activities and their satisfactory completion make us happy, whether or not they issue into anything that could be called "a pleasure."[4]

One might say that this kind of criticism is answered by a subtler form of hedonism, one that still uses pleasure as an ultimate principle but now recognizes that in our most rewarding experiences we do not treat it as a unitary goal. Still, many of our experiences cannot be categorized as either the having of pleasure or the lack of it. As I write these words, I am not aware of any pleasures that my writing affords to me. Nor does it seem adequate to say that writing is either pleasant, unpleasant, or something in between. The practice involves a certain amount of strain, anxiety, striving that is emotional, even physical, as well as cerebral. The experience is partly pleasant and partly unpleasant, like most of life. Despite the unpleasant parts, and incommensurate with the pleasant ones, I am eager to write whenever I can. Difficult as it is to write well, the attempt means a great deal to me. Whatever the incidental pleasures it may or may not give me, it provides some of the richest moments I can imagine.

When I think about the ingredients within the positive happiness that arises on such occasions, I find that even in the act of writing the intellect is only one among other relevant factors. As I have aged, it has become apparent to me that the vegetative aspects of our being have enormous importance in everything we do creatively. They are fundamental in our living happily and in our learning how to live. We tend to forget how much of human existence occurs at the vegetative level. Though we are not aware of them, our digestive juices are working constantly without needing mandates from our consciousness. Like plants and trees, we take in chemicals from the atmosphere without any prior thought. We likewise process and emit them in a cycle that requires no reflection. Much of our behavior is so habitual that the organism would seem to perform it automatically. The nonverbal and nonconceptual elements of the brain contribute to everything we say or think.

Despite the fact that our vegetative processes are always at work, we may not bestow value on them. Traditional religious dogmas have often sought to alienate us from these components of our being, either by denouncing "the body" or by considering it mechanical and therefore subhuman. But the vegetative is typically human. Though its function in us is less dominant than in plants or trees, it is as definitive of our nature as the rest of our complex state. We may or may not like the idea that we are partly vegetables. Yet our capacity for happiness largely hinges upon our acceptance of this datum.

When we are young and our purely intellectual powers are at their peak, we tend to identify them with problem solving. This attitude is entirely proper: without the ability to analyze experience and construct abstract theories, to formulate inductive and deductive arguments, there would be no science or philosophy. But eventually the probing spirit encounters barriers that may reveal to it how greatly any fruitful operation of the mind depends on sustenance from elements that are not themselves mental. In his book *The Conquest of Happiness* Bertrand Russell recommends an extrarational mode of dealing with whatever cognitive problems the intellect finds too unmanageable at the moment. He suggests that we deliberately bury such problems in our "unconscious" and leave instructions for the organism to solve them:

> My own belief is that a conscious thought can be planted into the unconscious if a sufficient amount of vigour and intensity is put into it. . . . I have found, for example, that if I have to write upon some rather difficult topic the best plan is to think about it with very great intensity—the greatest intensity of which I am capable—for a few hours or days, and at the end of that time give orders, so to speak, that the work is to proceed underground. After some months, I return consciously to the topic and find that the work has been done.[5]

The phrase "so to speak" is intriguing in this passage. The giving of orders is itself an act of consciousness, and one must wonder how the mind communicates with the unconscious powers that Russell specifies. I myself do not remember having ever made a decision, or given orders, such as those he mentions. Yet I recognize quite clearly the fermenting or gestating process to which he refers. For me, at least, it is a prerequisite for any creative work I do. Problems or puzzlements arise spontaneously, generally forced upon my consciousness by experiences of mine or else by events in my environment. Ideas occur as part of my need to make sense of the unresolved situation in which I find myself. I have no sensation of living in my mind alone, and my thinking does not exist within a realm of purely abstract reasoning. In order to encompass ideas that occupy, or rather *pre*occupy, me, my imagination seems to bring about a sinking into regions of myself that I cannot inspect and that scarcely respond to commands.

It is as if my conscious mind is the upper part of a plant that gets its nourishment from the soil in which it lives. Though the plant grows above the ground and reaches its own fulfillment by flowering or bearing fruit in the open air, it has no way of instructing the life-sustaining soil. The nutrients either come or they do not. The most one can do is to make oneself receptive, as the mystics report when they say their love of God consists in a willingness to let his love pour into them. What matters is the acceptance of our natural condition, the acceptance of our dependence upon our vital circumstance, the acceptance of the vegetative reality without which there can be neither life as we experience it nor any kind of happiness.

In his parallel account, Russell speaks of "the unconscious" in a manner that suggests the Freudian concept. But in Freud the unconscious is a region of the mind that follows laws of its own, which his putative science seeks to uncover. What I am describing is somewhat different. By "the vegetative" I refer to a part of our nature that is not unconscious mind but rather a concatenation of chemical and physiological processes. It resembles what Santayana calls "psyche," as contrasted with "spirit." I will return to Santayana's distinction in a later chapter. I mention it here because psyche, as Santayana defines it, belongs to the realm of matter. It is a nexus of physical and biological energy that enables an organism to survive in its environment.

When I experience the vegetative in myself, I do not feel that I have entered into a deeper level of my mind. On the contrary, it is as if I have brought to consciousness vital forces that permeate my body whether or not I am aware of them at any level. In my creative moments, on those occasions when my imagination is functioning efficiently, the ideas may even feel as if they are issuing from different parts of my body—from my lungs and diaphragm if I am speaking, from my knitted eyebrows when I try to think, or from my fingertips when I type on the keyboard of a computer. To get the spontaneity I seek in my writing, I let my fingers do the talking.

In moments such as these, various kinaesthetic sensations come to the fore as either the conveyors or the signals of generative powers churning within me. Renoir used to say that he painted with his penis. Several authors, for instance E. M. Forster, have spoken of their moments of inspiration as the lowering of a bucket into the well of their unconscious. This metaphor has always been troublesome for me. It is foreign to my own experience. I have generally felt that I myself am swimming in that fluid reservoir, and that far from lowering a bucket my imagination operates by opening my pores and allowing the enriching waters to penetrate as they wish.

If we accept the importance of our vegetative being, and above all if we value it as essential for our survival, like the air we breathe or the food we eat, we may come to relish faculties ordinarily taken for granted. One of these is memory. How wonderful it is to make present and immediate so many events that have long since disappeared. Everything may leave a trace in nature, but usually the lingering effect is slight and of minimal duration. Through memory, however, we are given a surrogate means of reliving our past experiences over and over again. Each time our remembrance reappears it will have been altered, somewhat distorted no doubt, often beautified by retroactive wish fulfillments, and almost always frayed or faded through attrition. But this is the price we must pay in order to keep the past alive. It must amalgamate itself with our present state of being, and that inevitably means a change from what it originally was. The process occurs spontaneously, through vegetative agencies about which we know very little. Our consciousness of memory is like the monitor of a computer. It shows forth the functions of recall lodged within our organic machine. Once we savor it as the marvelous attainment that it is, we can then enjoy moments in some previous experience that might otherwise have been destroyed completely.

I think it is the delight in cultivating this feat that explains why older men and women live with their memories so much more than do the young. One might say that the elderly have more of life to recall, and that they have less capacity to respond to present excitations because their vital energy has declined. But, human consciousness being what it is, there would seem to be a virtual infinity of events that one could remember at any age. And if older people cannot react to the present, how are they able to bring back the past so readily?

As everyone knows, the elderly often have difficulty remembering recent events even though their memory of those that are distant remains vivid and intact. It is as if the ability to store information diminishes with age but not the capacity to retrieve what was stored when we were young. The work of Hermann Ebbinghaus, and of more contemporary researchers in the field, indicates that one best remembers occurrences that are meaningful. For the old this often involves events that took place in earlier years, when their passions and sensory acuities were at a peak. The meaningful moments of the past have lingered with them and possibly been embellished through imaginative re-creation. The process becomes rewarding and benign only if we bestow greater value upon the mere phenomenon of memory as the years go by.

To make that bestowal we must accept, and even give ourselves to, the vegetative forces through which memory occurs. The anecdotage that many enjoy in old age manifests the way in which human beings create a meaning in their lives by virtue of memory alone. In time we become so enamored of our own experience that we learn how to regurgitate and to reenact it repeatedly. The ancient bore telling the same story for the hundredth time is like a glutton salivating over some cherished dish. To those who observe the spectacle, it may well seem like a revolting loss of human values. One becomes more tolerant, however, if one realizes that this individual is living in a gratifying rapport with powers that make it possible for life to continue in him or her. I do not mean that living in the past is preferable to living in the present as a wise or saintly person might. But wisdom and true saintliness also require an acceptance of oneself, including one's vegetative faculties.

Having established some communion with these organic elements that intellect has always scorned, we may thereby acquire a more extensive capacity for pleasure and even happiness. The routine acts of sex, locomotion, eating, defecation, or hearing, touching, smelling, seeing become consummatory when we accept them as signs that the body is doing what it naturally wants to do rather than carrying out tasks our mind has concocted for it. This greater delight is a recompense that we get for having learned how to live with our facticity as rooted though also mobile plants within whatever favorable soil we are lucky enough to have around us.

In living this way, we discover new opportunities for comfort and enjoyment. Where the younger person may have tossed and turned throughout a sleepless night, the older man or woman can possibly feel the pleasure that comes from lying on a good mattress, resting one's weary bones and overcharged intellect, whether or not one sleeps throughout the hours of darkness. In my own case, I think that some of the happiest moments of my life have occurred just before I fall asleep or wake up, when I linger in that twilight world between consciousness and unconsciousness, in a state of somnolent repose but also savoring the vital goodness of remaining this close to the vegetative in myself. As readers of *The Creation of Value* may remember, I have great difficulty in making sense out of Heidegger's notion of nothingness. The nearest I have come to understanding it happened when I fainted and apparently lay unconscious for several hours after having been in surgery. As I came to, I had the happy feeling that I was returning from total emptiness beyond any that I had known before. I do not think that this occurrence validates Heidegger's ontology, but in that brief experience I may have perceived the purely vegetative as it exists devoid of the usual encumbrances that mind imposes upon it.

Accepting life at this level may also have other consequences. Just as we can no longer treat animals of any sort as wound-up machinery once we share our lives with a domestic pet, so too we may feel that every tree and plant is kindred to us. We will not be able to exchange ideas with them, as we often do with cats and dogs, but we may be able to see them as living entities like ourselves. It is not necessary for us to embrace the magnificent beech or pine or oak trees that hover over our cottage. We recognize the differences that separate us from them. They will never acquire our kind of consciousness, and we will never revert to their mode of combining fixity with florescence. Despite the claims of Martin Buber, we can never hope to have what he called an "I-Thou" relationship with them. That is possible only with beings that have a self, and as far as we know, only animals do. These trees are just large plants. In the splendor of their healthy growth and adaptation to the environment, however, they display an achievement in life that we may well seek to emulate. That is the basis for our identification with them, and that is why we are able to love them. All of the contemporary concern about ecological preservation can be justified on these grounds alone.

If we now return to Schopenhauer's pendulum, we may find that we are better able to face the bleaker aspects of its dire pessimism. Though in a sense we are all prisoners of the random force that flows through nature, and though the oscillation between lack and satiety is a form of suffering that characterizes much of life, we are also sustained by material powers of which we are not always aware. Gravity serves to pull objects down, but simultaneously it gives them stability on earth without observable effort, as it also enables the earth to profit from its appointed orbit around the sun. To the degree that they are suitably used by living things, the laws of nature are fountainheads of organic fulfillment. Accepting them as what they are, we can employ them beneficially. The Furies then become Eumenides. They may not make us happy, but they bestow upon us the capacity for achieving happiness if only we live in accordance with our nature.

Happiness is therefore a positive accomplishment and not basically negative, as Schopenhauer thought. It is a state of consummation in which the different aspects of our being cooperate harmoniously. This may not be a very common occurrence, and it is never pure. It interweaves with meaningfulness in the devious ways I have been trying to analyze. To a large extent it depends on our ability to respond to the fact of mere existence. That is a concept I have touched upon in various places, and I return to it in later chapters of this book. My remarks about accepting the vegetative in ourselves may serve as a prelude to that discussion.

At the same time, we must not overemphasize the importance of the vegetative. We are also endowed with other animal faculties that conduce to our survival, and with intellectual aptitudes that often transcend their biological origins. Within our being as creatures in nature, we are able to have a life of spirit as well as materiality. An adequate perception of human happiness must take all these dimensions into account.

THE NATURE & CONTENT
OF HAPPINESS

❦

I began my discussion of happiness with Schopenhauer's pendulum theory because it is so radical a challenge to the common belief that a good life must be a happy one. As we saw, Schopenhauer insists not only that happiness is a very rare phenomenon but also that it runs counter to the fundamental structure of life. Yet all of Western philosophy, certainly from Aristotle onward, has been dominated by the idea that happiness is attainable as the reward for living as one should. In arguing against Schopenhauer, I have suggested that, far from being merely negative, happiness may serve as a fulfillment of our being and to that extent a contributor to the good life. But I have done little to explain the nature of this fulfillment, or of happiness itself. That is what I now wish to undertake.

Throughout my exploration I will be working with three different though joint concepts. As with all words that have great philosophic scope, *happiness* is richly ambiguous. I acknowledge this ambiguity, but I am not primarily interested in a semantic presentation of it. Without being exhaustive, the three concepts I analyze indicate what most philosophers have had in mind when they spoke about happiness as a human possibility. Individual thinkers prefer one or another of these notions, and their views are not necessarily compatible. They can nevertheless function as elements within a viable synthesis.

The first concept deals with happiness as a feeling. We speak, in fact, of people "feeling happy" on some occasion or at a specific time. Even when it lasts, the feeling of happiness is an episodic occurrence. Consider the following scene. You are walking through the park on a day in the spring. Apart from some puffy white clouds, the sky is blue. The sun shines brightly; the air is warm and it smells fresh; there is a slight breeze. Though you have responsibilities that must be attended to at the end of your walk, you do not give them any thought: you are aware only of how pleasant it is to be moving freely through this vernal setting. Each reader can imagine further details in accordance with his or her personal taste. Though the experience may be an isolated event within a hectic day, we can think of it as a time of happiness. In principle, at least, it could endure for quite a while.

The feeling of happiness can come upon us without preparation, without any apparent effort on our part, and in that sense, as a gratuitous phenomenon. But since it may not go on for very long, we need to distinguish between having a happy feeling and the having of a happy life. A life consists of many moments; a particular feeling need not occur in more than one of them. If a person feels happy on very few occasions, it would be odd to say that he has a happy life even if those occasions are temporally extensive. On the other hand, a happy life includes more than just the having of happy moments. And yet we can agree with philosophers, such as Bentham and James Mill, who believe that happiness itself should be defined in terms of a recognizable feeling, as in the example I have given.

In defending their idea of happiness, these philosophers usually mean that a happy life consists in a *predominance* of moments that yield a happy feeling. But how many are required for a life to be called a happy one? And how much of one's experience must they cover? At present we may ignore these questions. The crucial point is that happiness entails the having of feelings that are inherently gratifying, positive, and welcome to us whenever they do occur. A happy life is a life pervasively filled with happiness, and therefore it will often manifest these consummatory feelings.

For many people it makes sense intuitively to characterize

happiness as the ability to "enjoy" one's life. But the concept of enjoyment requires clarification, and I will return to that later. At this stage we need only mention it as an ingredient in happiness. Various thinkers have interpreted happiness-as-feeling to mean that we are "pleased" with our life, satisfied with it on balance and in its totality. This is an alternate, though closely related, way of describing feelings that the notion of happiness may entail. Though feeling good about one's life is only one among other happy feelings that we might have, it can possibly tell us something about the nature of happiness.[1]

In this first conception, then, happiness is either a specific event—one or another feeling—or else a composite of them throughout a lifetime. The second approach analyzes happiness in terms of processes that belong to our condition as organisms struggling to survive and to prosper within the natural environment. Happiness, whether it exists for a short period or for many years, is taken to be a matter of functioning effectively. We all have desires, and we all wish to satisfy them; we engage in purposive activities designed to get whatever we want in conformity with one or another system of values that guides our behavior; when these efforts succeed and our aspirations are fulfilled, we experience happiness as a manifestation of the fact that we are in tune with nature and our organic being. In that sense happiness is the ultimate goal toward which our endeavors were all directed.

From this point of view, which was Aristotle's, happiness emanates from the human capacity to actualize our natural potentialities, to succeed as functioning instances of our species, to act well rather than to feel good. A happy life is one in which the process of search and attainment is renewed continuously, or else with adequate frequency despite occasional lapses that occur in its normal operation. At stake is much more than just the having of felicitous sensations, since the appropriate attunement involves activities that may have to be strenuous, wearisome, even unpleasant at times.

In this vein, philosophers sometimes define happiness as "attitudinal." But that might be misleading. Being happy is not the same as having a happy disposition, although the latter facilitates the former. If one has the requisite attitude, happiness can be easier to attain. What we attain, however, is not just an attitude. However desirable it may be, a happy disposition must issue into coordinated activities that finally reach completion and provide related consummations of one sort or another.

The third conception differs from the first two in identifying happiness with good fortune. That may be the oldest meaning of the word, and in fact it appears as the first definition in the *Oxford English Dictionary*. We can all agree that happy people are fortunate in being happy, but there is also the idea that something in the *nature* of happiness involves good fortune. We speak of a happy idea or a happy turn of events, meaning that the outcome is favorable and implying that chance has something to do with it. So too can we say that a happy person is one who has the good luck to be well constituted for life in his or her immediate environment. There is a kind of natural harmony or grace that results from having traits and talents that are valued by the parents to whom we were born and the society in which we were reared. It is always a matter of happenstance that a child with one or another set of innate capacities should have come into existence when and where it does. Some people seem to have been born happy. It is as if they, at least, were made for happiness. Others seem to have been doomed in advance. And even the happiest of men and women transplanted to a barren or forbidding environment would no longer be happy. Their happiness depends on the good fortune of being able to live in a world that is receptive to their inclinations and their personal welfare.

In relation to this third concept, we may wonder whether it elucidates the nature of happiness rather than conditions under which someone can be happy. Unless people had reasonably good fortune, one might say, they could not experience happiness. In a wholly unfavorable setting or ravaged by unbearable constraints, no one would be happy. But can this signify what happiness *is*, by definition and in itself? Should we not conclude that the third concept has a different logical status?

An argument along these lines seems to me quite plausible prima facie. One assumes that happiness must either be something felt or else a pattern of self-realization. Having the good fortune to be wanted and at home in one's environment may only be a prerequisite for happiness to occur, which is not the same as explicating its nature. Nevertheless, we might argue that happiness is simply this gratuitous sense of oneness between our individual being and our circumstances. Without stretching ordinary language very far, we could assert that happiness consists in living in a world that recurrently welcomes our existence. The happy man or woman is thus the one who is lucky enough to have appetites and interests that nature and society are willing to accept and often gratify.

✳

Without trying to resolve this technical issue, I will proceed on the assumption that the third concept helps us to understand the meaning of happiness. I believe that the three ideas supplement one another. Each requires further clarification, but all of them are needed for an adequate analysis.

The first concept derives from our established belief that happiness refers to feeling good *in* our life and *about* our life. We would never think of ascribing happiness to inanimate objects. Indeed, it is unlikely that anyone would imagine it occurring in forms of life that are not conscious or have no experience. If we say that the geranium in the window box is not happy to be watered by acid rain, we are talking metaphorically. We do not mean that the geranium is unhappy in the same sense in which starving or malnourished humanity is unhappy. We mean only that the plant is undergoing something harmful to its existence. That is analogous to the condition of human beings who are deprived of food, but what the geranium and these people have in common is not a state of unhappiness. In part at least, that state is a feeling within consciousness, which plants presumably do not have.

Similarly, it would be odd to say that someone in a coma is either happy or unhappy. As far as we can tell, this person is then not having any feelings. But what if we were sure the unconscious patient has sensations of some kind though we cannot tell whether they are enjoyable? That would not be enough if we wished to determine whether the person is happy or unhappy. Happiness pertains to feelings that one *enjoys* having; a happy life can include periods of unconsciousness—for instance, when we sleep each night—but it must be a life in which we are consciously pleased by our existence, abundantly and on many occasions.

How much enjoyment must there be? One is tempted to answer: the more the better, as far as happiness is concerned. But does that mean a life of continuous and unadulterated enjoyment would be the happiest one? The concept of "bliss" is reserved for this imagined possibility. Some people anticipate it as a reward they will receive in heaven. It is not, however, an idea that is congruent with happiness on earth. For us happiness is a state that we can experience only in the world we know and within the confines of our natural being. As such, it cannot be either continuous or unadulterated. The notion of perfect bliss is just a figment, gratifying perhaps as make-believe but deceptive about our reality.

Other questions attend the idea that happiness is nothing but enjoyable feeling. What exactly, we may ask, is the nature of a feeling of enjoyment? Some philosophers claim it is the experience of pleasure. But that is usually interpreted as a sensory event that is localizable in one or another part of the body, as physical pains always are. If this is what we mean by pleasure, we cannot think that it alone reveals the nature of happiness. As moralists have often pointed out, pursuing and securing pleasures is not the same as pursuing and securing happiness. Sybarites have a highly cultivated taste for pleasurable possibilities. They seek experiences and activities for no reason other than their ability to afford them pleasures that they value. One might say that this is the exclusive means by which they are able to enjoy life. To know whether they are happy, however, we would need to determine whether their lives are enjoyable as a whole. The mere having of pleasure is not enough. We usually want much more than that.

The sybarites might tell us that they do not. And in their case bountiful pleasures, however limited in scope, may well be the means by which a kind of happiness is procured. For others, people who have neither the interests nor the peculiar talents of a sybarite, life can be enjoyed without a great quantity of pleasurable experiences. Far from being deprived of happiness, nonsybarites may often have a happier life than those who are sybaritic. The search for maximum pleasurability can be hard work, even for someone who is suitably motivated, and many people find that existence becomes more enjoyable when they resist the lure of pleasure and avoid the laborious pursuit of it.

At the same time, there must be some connection between the having of pleasures and the experience of happiness. If someone lived with no pleasures of any kind, could we possibly consider that person happy? I do not think so. Still, we cannot specify *how much* pleasure is essential for happiness to exist, or how intense one's pleasures must be, or even how frequently they need occur. The most we can say is that no one could be happy unless he or she had pleasures adequate for that person's enjoyment of life. The actual amount or quality will vary tremendously from individual to individual.

In studying this first conception of happiness, we need to recognize the vagueness and the looseness of our language. I have been distinguishing between enjoyment and pleasure. But what are we to say about terms like *pleasantness* or expressions like *being pleased with one's existence*? A pleasant life is one that is mild, moderate in its quantity of enjoyability, far from being ecstatic but generally immune to distasteful effects of violent passion. We associate merely pleasant experience with contentment rather than happiness. But possibly contentment is a form of happiness, a calmer version of it, just as joy can be interpreted as focused or ecstatic happiness. The manic quality of unbounded joyfulness is different from the quietude of contentment without necessarily preventing either from being a type of happiness.

If a person says that he is pleased with his life, we recognize that he is satisfied to exist as he does. Should we then conclude that he experiences the enjoyment needed for happiness? Possibly not, for one may be pleased and satisfied in this way without realizing how little one is getting out of life. In order to escape these difficulties in distinguishing between pleasure, having pleasant experiences, and being pleased with one's existence, many philosophers prefer to identify happiness with the repeated occurrence of a "positive hedonic tone." That has the virtue of being a general and amorphous term, but it is not very helpful: it adds scarcely anything to what we already mean by enjoyment as an element in experience.

However we interpret the meaning of enjoyment, the first conception is inadequate by itself. We have already gone beyond it in perceiving that even pure and endless bliss would not explain the happiness that is relevant to our nature as human beings. But while the idea of bliss may be discarded as a valid clue to our kind of happiness, there are other states that may seem to be more plausible. Consider Elwood P. Dowd, the serenely cheerful man in the play and movie *Harvey*, who enjoys the company of a six-foot three-inch rabbit visible to no one else. The humorous situations that ensue presuppose that the audience naturally assumes no such rabbit exists. During most of the comedy we are intrigued by the fact that, despite his major delusion, Dowd, and only he, is likable, humane, sensible, and well tempered. He is a happy man, and the other characters, all of them sane, are far from being happy. At the end, we are given a glimpse of the rabbit, and the others see him too, as a wry suggestion that possibly loonies like Dowd can find happiness based on realities hidden from the rest of us.

I mention this particular instance because it illustrates a frequent belief that people who have benign hallucinations and live in "a world of their own" may often be happier than other men and women. In our bondage to everyday cares, we may even feel a bit envious of the smiling village idiot who seems completely happy sitting in the sun and doing nothing. Those who have convinced themselves that they are Napoleon or Jesus Christ inflate their own importance by blotting out everything that can undermine the enjoyability of their private fantasies. And if the environment cooperates, if the world humors them in their madness, this maneuver may sometimes work. But are such people *really* happy, and are we willing to treat their condition as definitive of the happiness that others may also experience? By employing the second conception as well as the first, we acknowledge that something more than mere enjoyment is needed for a happy life.

For its part, the second concept of happiness is problematic precisely because it does go beyond the hedonic quality. One is tempted to say that the village idiot or hebephrenic dreamer is at a disadvantage not because he lacks happiness but rather because his life has no meaning. But if we define happiness by reference to successful pursuit of goals that satisfy our desires and fulfill our organic needs, as the second concept does, are we not conflating happiness with meaningfulness? Having argued that these should be distinguished from each other, am I not being inconsistent in now admitting criteria of happiness that are themselves dependent on meaning?

I think the answer must be no. Happiness and meaningfulness are interwoven, but they are not the same. Meaningful lives are often troublesome, anxious, and wracked by indecision and self-doubt. One thinks of Michelangelo or Beethoven as persons who had a life filled with meaning. We would hardly say that their existence is paradigmatic of happiness. And yet they must also have had happy, indeed joyful moments that most of us cannot approximate. Certainly they were happy when they achieved artistic goals for which they had striven. With their enormous creativity, they experienced, on some occasions at least, a kind of ecstasy unknown to other people. But geniuses like them are so constituted that they refuse to savor or preserve their feelings of happiness. They may even reject them as being subversive to what matters most. They orient their entire being toward new and increasingly difficult projects without wanting, or being able, to relish the fruits of their past successes. Whether or not we call such behavior pathological, we must recognize that it contributes to heroic meaningfulness that may never culminate in a happy life.

Meaning and happiness are interrelated insofar as a wholly meaningless life would not be a happy one for most and possibly all human beings. But there is no reason to assume that the more meaningful a life becomes the more it leads to happiness. What makes life meaningful for some individuals may cause them to sacrifice their own happiness. In the best of all possible worlds, that would not occur. In ours it often does.

A life that is completely boring or devoid of enjoyment will not be experienced as having any meaning. And if a life had no meaning, it would lack the kind of happiness that most people cherish. For life to manifest either happiness or meaningfulness, it must normally include challenges and decisions, goals and aspirations, purposes and consummatory experiences derivative from those purposes. It must be a life that has been chosen by the person who is living it—not only chosen in its entirety but also as it is lived from moment to moment. Robert Nozick rightly argues that for most people an "experience machine" would be unacceptable if it automatically made them feel happy, or even blissful, without their doing anything to bring this feeling into being other than starting the mechanism once and for all. Enjoyable as our experience might be as long as the machine continues to operate, we could never believe that we are living our own lives and making them meaningful through our own consecutive choices. The sense of freedom, the feeling that our experience depends on decisions we ourselves have made, would be lacking.[2]

To the extent that we have a life of meaning, we create our own destiny. It is hard to believe that anyone can be fully happy without that awareness. Happiness requires at least a modicum of meaning in the lives that human beings both create and know they are creating through their own explicit efforts. This necessary ingredient is fully recognized by the second concept.

Where the first conception emphasized the importance of enjoyment, the second one stresses self-realization and the satisfaction of need or desire. We do not have to single out some preferential desires rather than others. What matters most is for people to pursue interests that they really care about. Nor is satisfaction uniquely paramount in itself. The satisfying of a desire is the completing of a vital episode that includes an appetitive impulse, the search for valued goals or objects, and the fulfillment of one or another purpose. Each of these elements, including the culminating satisfaction, is but an integral part of a continuous process that directs one's energies as required by the circumstances.

To this extent, the happy man or woman is the one whose relationship with the environment is so harmonious that the overall transaction feels and *becomes* efficacious. It is hard to imagine a life that would be enjoyable from beginning to end, but we can readily conceive of a life that consists of meaningful interaction with our surroundings as the basis for satisfying whatever desires arise in us. In this process spirit issues out of nature while also creating in it value that would not otherwise exist. Religious mythology provides an image of this harmony between spirit and the natural world in that idea I mentioned earlier of God's foot activating the treadle of the universe. With or without its transcendental implications, that is the model of happiness to which the second concept adheres.

※

The third concept intersects the first and second, but it too has problems of its own. I used it when I just spoke about harmony with the environment. Insofar as we do have a harmonious relationship with our surroundings, we are the beneficiaries of unpredictable good fortune. There is little we can ultimately do to make the universe a place in which our desires will find the home they are always seeking. Though we are the children of nature and the particularized expressions of whatever culture has molded our feelings and our intellect, we are also castaways separated from natural as well as social origins by our idiosyncratic tastes and predilections. There is no reason to assume a priori that our multiple yearnings will be greeted by the environment in which they occur. That is largely a matter of chance that lies beyond any purposive efforts we can make.

Happy is the person who lives at the right time, in the right place, and who brings to the world in which he lives the right talents or capacities—the ones that his contemporaries can recognize and appreciate. He will not be happy unless they both need and want what he can provide. But this must always depend on the luck of the draw. It is what we call fate, or kismet, or God's inscrutable will.

The inherent difficulties of the third concept appear most dramatically in something Aristotle said when he wondered whether everyone can be happy. In the *Nicomachean Ethics* he argues that by their very constitution some people are incapable of attaining *eudaimonia* (usually translated as "happiness"). He mentions those who are slaves by nature, but he would also include children and retarded men and women. What makes someone a slave, according to Aristotle, and what applies to these other persons as well, is a constant inability to plan one's life through rational deliberation. Since Aristotle believes that virtue requires the proper use of practical reason, and since he cannot imagine happiness occurring without virtue, he has no difficulty in limiting his conception of the happy life as he does. Happiness would seem to be a matter of having the good luck that natural slaves or retarded individuals will never have, and that children can only hope to experience at some time in their future development.

Though Aristotle is ambiguous in what he means by "natural" slaves, we may interpret him as referring to people whose constitutional weakness of intellect or will renders them inferior to those who are masters of their fate and vigorously devote themselves to what is good in life. But are we prepared to say that only strong-minded persons can be truly happy? Though rationality and intestinal fortitude are gifts of nature that buttress the happiness of those who have them, are such virtues more essential than a sunny outlook and compliant acquiescence to the given order of things? These traits may also depend on good fortune. And are they not needed, as much as rationality, if we are to enjoy whatever life we have?

I can illustrate this problem by considering the situation of Piccarda in Dante's *Paradiso*. Inveterate Platonist that he is, Dante has all along believed that salvation consists in getting as close as possible to the Good, that is, God. He thinks that it is in the nature of everyone to strive for this, and he assumes that happiness will always be proportionate to the degree of proximity one is able to achieve. But in the sphere of the moon, which is located near the outer limits of paradise and is therefore somewhat remote from the divine center, he encounters the infinitely joyful spirit of Piccarda.

When he asks her whether her happiness is not marred by the fact that she has been stationed so far away from God, she denies that the quality of her bliss is at all impaired. It is by accepting God's will in these matters, she explains, that spirits like herself find their absolute peace.

Despite the puzzlement this occasions in Dante, we may surely agree with Piccarda's claim that people like her can be extremely happy. Theirs will be a happiness different from the kind that Aristotle prefers and yet as real as any other. But Piccarda's complacent acceptance of her lot is also dependent on good fortune. Those who have a less accommodating temperament, or a different upbringing, both of which are largely out of their control, will not experience the world the way she does. Variable as it may be, the happy life always involves some fortunate relation to our immediate surroundings. However widely we throw the net of happiness, we must still recognize that each instance involves preconditions that the person who is happy cannot entirely determine. Piccarda was born under a lucky star, just as Beatrice in Shakespeare's *Much Ado about Nothing* says her merry disposition comes from having been born under a star that danced. Piccarda's bliss resides in her ability to accept God's will, but that ability is the product of an attitude that God (or nature) has already willed in her.

Should we say, then, that the third concept necessarily conflicts with the second? To the extent that we are happy only if our existence is harmonious with our environs in ways that we ourselves do not establish, our happiness depends on something other than the living of a life that we have chosen. Aristotle's happy man did not decide to be a person who can use his reason in a constructive manner that satisfies his virtuous desires. Although he is responsible for cultivating that purposive aptitude in himself, as he is also responsible for the choices he makes, he is not responsible for having this or any other talent in the first place.

We should not infer, however, that the two ideas of happiness are mutually inconsistent. On the contrary, they supplement each other. The same holds for the relationship between either of these concepts and the first one. By using all three, we get a richer insight into the nature and content of happiness than we would if we limited ourselves to one of them. Though they diverge, they also form a unity among themselves.

❋

I do not wish to suggest that this harmonization must always combine the different elements uniformly. In ordinary discourse the word *happiness* often serves to emphasize one or another without much regard about the other two. As philosophers we are entitled, even required, to envisage modes of thought that are more coherent and precise than those that everyday language conveys. But it would be a mistake to suggest an analysis that is too constraining or procrustean. The most we can say is that all three conceptions should make their individual contribution to our thinking about happiness.

A life we may plausibly denote as happy is one that remains enjoyable through much of its duration and, not infrequently, provides moments of pleasure. How often must there be this feeling of enjoyment? How intense must it be? How greatly must it include pleasurability, and of what sort? These questions are not inappropriate, but they are all unanswerable. Happiness will not be the same for any two persons. We may also leave in abeyance quandaries about the gray area between pleasure and pain. In the Gilbert and Sullivan opera *Patience* a sextet of lovers sing that they can now rejoice because "The pain [in their previously frustrated longing] that is all but a pleasure will change / For the pleasure that's all but pain." A happy life would not be one that is largely or purely painful, but the quality and quantity of the pleasures, or pleasurable pains, which it may include can vary tremendously.

Moreover, our paradigm must also contain components that are not directly related to the hedonic. For happiness to exist there must be a sense of meaning in much of what we do or feel, and a self-assurance (which I elsewhere call self-love or faith in oneself) that strengthens whatever activities we pursue in a purposive manner. To some extent, our efforts must be satisfying in themselves as well as in the experiences to which they lead. Though we recognize that all existence is subject to the vicissitudes of unmanageable forces in nature, we may nevertheless feel that we are happy only in living a life we have freely chosen as our own.

And finally, our enlarged model will integrate not just the hedonic and the purposive but also the element of fortuitous attunement with an environment that is receptive toward our being. To one who has this good fortune, the experience of happiness may appear as amazing grace. Even so, much of this serendipity depends on our doing what is needed to get the self-fulfillment that we want, which is why the third ingredient must enter into unity with the first two. Though seeming to be different, the environment that supports us is the same as the one we struggle with in the hope of wringing from it enjoyable experiences and the satisfaction of needs. When all goes well, as it does in moments of happiness, we sense the power and aggrandizement that come from having imposed our will. But we may also intone *"non nobis"* and feel a further happiness in believing that God or Nature or Dame Fortune has contrived to make it possible for us to have any goodness at all. We thereby voice the fundamental faith without which life is not worth living.

However coherent in its broadest outlines this composite theory of happiness may be, there are two kinds of philosophers who will find it inadequate. The first kind, represented by John Stuart Mill, thinks of happiness as the exclusive and all-inclusive goal of human conduct. As such, happiness is considered not only the highest ideal but also one that subsumes within itself, either directly or indirectly, all other aspects of the good life. The second countervening approach, which Aristotle preeminently illustrates, maintains that happiness must be defined in terms of a specific faculty, in his case rationality conducive to practical virtue. Each of these positions is essentialistic in a way that I have been systematically avoiding. In view of what I have said about the diversity of ideals that matter to human beings, and about the plurality of lives that may be meaningful and equally happy, there is no need for me to repeat my reasons for rejecting both philosophies.

At this juncture, we may be poised at one of those crucial forks in deliberation where additional argument becomes fruitless. Eventually one must harken to one's own intuition of what the world is like and what contributes to a good life. People with experience and a temperament that is not the same as mine might very well prefer the perspectives of either Mill or Aristotle. After examining the concept of nature and what it means to live in accordance with it, I may be able to resolve a few of our differences. In the concluding chapter I offer some observations about the limits of any actual happiness. But first I wish to explore the possibility that concepts of play or mere existence can amplify the preliminary definition I have given here.

4

PLAY & MERE EXISTENCE

However open and incomplete our discussion of happiness may be, it should enable us to deal with some of the practical questions that people ask. For instance, what can one do to be happy? Can happiness be stultifying? Is it more likely to occur at one time of life rather than another, and in which society or relationship? Having criticized Schopenhauer's assertion that authentic happiness is foreign to our nature, can we believe—as Wittgenstein suggested—that it reveals the purpose of life itself? These questions are not entirely separate from one another, and they obviously overlap with problems about the nature of purpose or meaning. In the next few pages I try to provide some tentative answers.

It is often said that we can be happy only if we take life "as it comes, day by day." The gospels advise us to have no thought of the morrow and to emulate birds of the air, which "sow not, neither do they reap." The idea is that we can live on faith, as others have claimed that men and women can live on love alone. And surely it is true that faith or love may yield the happiness of thinking that all is for the best, either in the universe or in our personal relations. If only we can slough away the incrustations of worldly cares and avoidable distractions, would we not revert to a life in which happiness will naturally issue forth? Some have described this beneficent state as the ability to play, which children possess supremely, while others have recommended a quasi-mystical acceptance of mere existence.

Both suggestions may strike us as implausible and even counter-intuitive. Children play as they do because they are learning how to live in the world; they are experimenting with life; they are developing, through trial and error, faculties that will enable them to thrive as they grow up. Even if they are sometimes happy at this early stage, why think that their mode of being reveals what is needed for happiness in general? As for living at the level of mere existence, does this not characterize the condition of someone who has nothing to live *for*? He or she would seem to be unengaged, inert, and not truly happy. Both this person and the one who plays at everything are like a ship that drifts and must eventually founder. Unless there is something that matters to them, we may feel, they will find neither happiness nor meaning in their lives. Happiness results not from the avoidance of purposive activities but rather from their amelioration and enrichment. The play and mere existence theses appear to ignore this fact.

Still, each of them is worth examining. One of the most trenchant defenses of play as the source of both happiness and meaning occurs in an article that the Austrian philosopher Moritz Schlick wrote in the 1930s. Schlick was concerned about the extent to which contemporary men and women devote their energies to productive work without ever really enjoying life. He defined work as behavior that "has its purpose outside itself, and is not performed for its own sake."[1] Schlick argued that Schopenhauer's mistake consisted in thinking that happiness depends on obtaining a satisfaction that eliminates prior or preliminary desires, whereas it actually involves the having of feelings, and the performing of activities, that are satisfying in themselves. Since purposiveness usually requires us to subordinate present interests for the sake of ulterior goals, Schlick claims it is only when we liberate ourselves from the primacy of goal orientation and learn how to enjoy each moment as it passes that we can make life happy as well as meaningful. He proffers the following "highest rule of action": "What is not worth doing for its own sake, don't do for anything else's sake!"[2]

Schlick associates the ability to enjoy life with an attitude of playfulness. He sees play as inherently a mode of living that transcends the restraints of mere purposiveness. Through play we undergo each momentary occurrence for its own sake; we then have access to rewarding possibilities without deferring them until some distant end has been attained. At the same time Schlick insists that a playful disposition is wholly compatible with working toward desired goals. For though the outcome of our labor may be useful in various ways, we may nevertheless treat the purposive activities as a kind of play. Schlick thinks this is the ideal that humanity should pursue, and he suggests that all creativity—whether in art or science—is playful as well as productive.

Schlick correctly perceives that creative people do what they do because they enjoy their capacity to play with reality, however it presents itself. The means then become ends, and that can extend throughout one's life and regardless of what one's individual talents may happen to be. Since creative experience can occur in the doing of what is needed for human welfare or personal benefit, there is no basic incompatibility in living for the moment with a playful attitude while also acting to achieve purposive goals. Playfulness in no way prevents us from getting the goods of life that everyone seeks.

Schlick identifies play with the initial stages of human development, and he laments the traditional idea that youth is mainly a time of preparation for adulthood. On the contrary, he says, children know better than their elders how to live, insofar as children treat all life as play and have not yet been corrupted by the deadening need to behave in accordance with one or another of the standards that society will someday force upon them. But while he glorifies the young in this respect, Schlick claims that older people can have a residual youthfulness that enables them to play creatively regardless of their age. He asserts that "the meaning of life is youth," but he also holds that youth "is present wherever the state of man has reached a peak, where his action has become play, where he is wholly given over to the moment and the matter in hand."[3]

We may say, then, that Schlick is advocating playfulness that first appears in childhood but also recurs as that which gives value to the activities of later life. Wholly immersed in the present, the playful person can pursue purposive ends without being dominated by them. Relishing the values of playfulness, he or she is free to act with utmost creativity.

Schlick's account seems faulty to me. Though he does well to emphasize the importance of play in both children and adults, he fails to recognize that when children engage in it they are often playing at being adults who seem to them remarkably successful in carrying out their purposive intentions. Much of the time, play consists in a progressive acquisition of skills that the child needs in order to grow into adequate maturity. To a large degree, childhood play is part of a learning process that helps the young to acquire capabilities they themselves exorbitantly value.

Following a long tradition of romanticism dating back at least to the beginning of the nineteenth century, Schlick idealizes the carefree insouciance of children as if this were all that either play or playfulness involves. He even quotes, approvingly, Schiller's remark that it is through "idleness and indifference" that the Greek gods achieve their sublime state of being. When we are idle and indifferent, our experience has detached itself from the purposive life. But playfulness, in young as well as older human beings, is not like that. It generally contains a great many purposes of its own, albeit purposes that have been constructed as variations on, or even deviations from, the goal-oriented behavior needed for staying alive.

Schlick is right in suggesting that the ideal would be a harmonization between play and purpose. That is why he cites the creative playfulness of great artists and extols acts that are undertaken for some useful end while also remaining enjoyable. He calls this a "transformation of the means into an end-in-itself," and he sees that almost any interest can be made amenable to such transformation. What he does not wholly recognize is the fact that means can be satisfying not only as ends but also *as means*. In his eagerness to recommend patterns of life that are thoroughly enjoyable, consummatory in their components as well as in the results to which they lead, Schlick ignores the possibility that happy lives must also include valued instrumentalities that would not be cherished other-wise. These can be desired, and a source of gratification, *because* we know they are the means by which we obtain ends that matter to us.

I am suggesting, therefore, that much of happiness involves a kind of fulfillment that cannot be explained by the concept of play-fulness alone. The delighting in means that we perceive as means only, and not as ends, is an important consideration even in child-hood play. Children love to see that what they do really *works*, that it has consequences they have brought about, that it changes the world and makes it conform to their demands. Purposefulness, when it succeeds and is suitably enacted, contributes to self-realization as much as—and sometimes more than—playfulness that is idle, in-different, or autotelic. Play of that sort can strike us as frivolous and even silly, to use a word that children frequently employ in this context. Children are very perceptive, even wise, in their scorn for the silliness of grown-ups. They intuit that such people are doing something in a misguided attempt to imitate childhood play. The children know from experience how thoroughly their own playful attitude depends on the purposive elements within it.

On the other hand, playfulness itself does not occur fully per-fected in childhood. It too develops over a period of time and often flourishes as the expression of a person's ability to survive in the purposeful world that adults experience. This development requires a significant degree of maturity. Though youth may not be wasted on the young, as G. B. Shaw thought, its basic goodness may appear only after one realizes in later life how much of playfulness is linked to whatever purposive capacities one has acquired over the years.

I conclude that the concept of play, at least as it is formulated by philosophers like Schiller and Schlick, cannot yield everything we have to know about either happiness or a meaningful life.

As an alternate way of engaging related problems, we may wonder why it is that so many people value mere existence. In *The Creation of Value* I criticized Thomas Nagel's assumption that the having of experience is a good that can in itself outweigh all the bad elements that may belong to someone's life. This belief led Nagel to infer that death, which eliminates our mere existence, is always an evil or misfortune. More recently, Richard Wollheim has made a similar assertion.[4] Arguing that the quality of experience depends on the relative goodness or badness of its contents, I claimed that death is not an evil if the bad elements predominate and one's life becomes sufficiently unbearable.[5]

The fact remains, however, that most people want to go on living indefinitely, and often regardless of the misery or general suffering that they would undergo. Mere existence means so much to us that we cling to it even when a rational weighing of good against bad elements would indicate that we do better to exist no longer. The fear of death, which everyone has felt at some time or other, is a fear that we will not only lose the good things in life but also be deprived of our mere existence. Staying alive, in and by itself, would seem to be an ultimate and irreducible value. And if that is true, the vivid realization that one does exist, and will go on doing so, might have special importance in the attainment of happiness.

Studying this possibility, we do well to examine the hunger for immortality that is so common among human beings. That craving frequently reduces to little more than an abstract desire for existence that never ends. It is natural and normal for living things to want to enjoy whatever goods the world has been affording them. But the longing for immortality implies something further. It is generally predicated upon the feeling that life is a goodness in itself and therefore worth extending regardless of its qualitative merit.

As a casual hope or aspiration, the dream of immortality need not be attacked. It is a product of the same imaginative faculty that makes one want to be much brighter or more creative than one is. Problems arise when we ask what it really would be like to live forever, and whether mere existence contributes much to either happiness or meaning. To prove that "an endless life would be a meaningless one," Bernard Williams cites the legendary Makropulos case.[6] Having drunk an elixir that keeps her from aging, Elina Makropulos exists for centuries in a state of boredom and joylessness. She has outlived not only the generation to which she was born but also a series of later ones in which her experiences keep repeating themselves with ever increasing tedium. Given what it is to be a human being, Williams claims, immortality must always lead to calamity of that sort.

Jonathan Swift had a similar idea about the inevitable limitations of life. In *Gulliver's Travels* he depicts the Struldbrugs as a breed of cursed individuals who live forever but degenerate physically and mentally, becoming more and more of a burden to their society and a horror to themselves. Throughout the many years of her continuing existence, Elina Makropulos stays at her original age of forty-two, and Williams himself considers this "an admirable age" at which to remain unendingly. Nevertheless he is convinced that, even at its best, no time of life and no human circumstance could surmount the dreary repetitiveness resulting from immortality.

In the fable of Baron Munchausen we encounter a different perspective on longevity. Having done a service for the magician Cagliostro, Munchausen is offered anything he desires. He requests, and receives, the ability to live as he is for as long as he wants and to die whenever he so ordains. He is in his middle to late twenties, and he enjoys the pleasures of youthfulness for many years at that age. After a succession of satisfying amatory adventures, he falls in love with a woman from whom he cannot bear to be separated. When she approaches death, he forfeits immortality. He chooses to die rather than to live without her.

One might interpret this fable as signifying that love is stronger than the craving for mere existence, stronger even than the possibility of happiness apart from love. The case of Baron Munchausen is worth mentioning here because it illustrates a way out of the predicament posed by Swift and Williams. Although we can readily envisage human life turning into boredom and misery when it lasts beyond our ability to have enjoyable experience, we also respond to the notion that life is worth prolonging indefinitely under optimal conditions. If, like Munchausen before he fell in love, we could always be young and engulfed in pleasures that remain unsullied by doubt or difficulty, would we not feel that happiness resides in the mere continuance of that existence? And if the person we love, and our friends and everyone else we care about, could have a similar immortality, would this not provide endless happiness?

Many people would say so. But neither this nor any of the previous accounts seems persuasive to me. They do not explain why existence should be idealized, and neither do they reveal what is deepest in our hopes for immortality. In wanting to live without ever dying, we want to stay as we are—but not in the sense of being arrested at any moment in life, however happy or consummatory that moment may be. It is true that we wish to preserve the identity of "ourselves," and at each point we think of our self in terms of what we have become and now are. But we are what we are because we have lived through all the intervening stages that make up our existence in the present. Our experience is the upshot of vital processes through which we have developed and will do so in the future. Our faculties and strength of enjoyment are always diminishing in some respects but also evolving in various directions that may not yet be apparent to us.

As long as we are healthy in mind and body, we can easily tolerate the fact that former satisfactions are no longer available. They will have been replaced by new ones more congruent with our place within the ongoing process. If we remained at a particular age, like either Baron Munchausen or Elina Makropulos, we could not experience the incremental happiness that human beings crave. If we deteriorate, like the Struldbrugs or like the never dying protagonist in Aldous Huxley's *Eyeless in Gaza*, that too rules out an immortality that we would deem desirable. What we really want is to *improve* forever, enjoying life as we have throughout the best periods in the past but also renewing it unceasingly as a changing vitality that moves us into novel opportunities for continuous self-creation. These may lie beyond our current ability, and they will surely exceed our powers of imagination. But since the developmental process will be the one in which we have always existed, we can feel that our life without death is indeed an immortality worth possessing.

In saying this, I realize that the yearning for immortal life has usually presented itself in a different guise. Traditional religions have often disprized the body, at least as it exists in its natural state.

They have most often promised immortality only for the mind or spirit. Such doctrines are perplexing, since we have no acquaintance with minds or spirits apart from bodies. We do have immediate experience of a consciousness that *feels* as if it might be separable from its material embodiment. But we have no way of validating this feeling.

Even the desire for immortality as I have described it will seem unrealistic to some people. Indeed, the vital forces that operate in us are notoriously short-lived. They depend on a fragile environment located within the confines of this particular planet, and on chemical and organic combinations that do not exist for very long. And while it is true that aging men and women acquire—if they are lucky— new aptitudes that partly compensate them for the decline of earlier ones, the entire trajectory occurs within a constant diminution of the physical resources required for any existence whatsoever.

We might reply to this criticism by remarking that technology may someday transform our present expectations about the quality and duration of life. If not on this planet, then possibly on some other, we may eventually be able to live much longer than we now do. Immortal life may be harder to imagine. But perhaps we can see immortality as an indefinite span whose termination is so remote that we cannot envisage it with any clarity. And since our knowledge about the universe is very meager, we may speculate that life without death might conceivably include the evolution of nonterminating creatures different from, but similar to, ourselves.

Despite these emendations, however, we should still distrust the usual hunger for mere existence. That alone does not guarantee either a happy or a meaningful life. On the contrary, it is always our desire for happiness, meaning, or love which gives value to existence. In itself, life has no special goodness. Those who speak of the pleasure, the delight, "just in being alive" are attesting not to the goodness of existence but rather to their good fortune in having lives that are worth living, lives that are enjoyable or filled with meaning. When he was ninety-something, the comedian George Burns said as he appeared on stage: "I'm glad to be here. At my age I'm glad to be anywhere." I do not think he would have said that, and I am sure the audience would not have responded as it did, if he were in a state of agony.

Existence is a prior condition for happiness, but only in the trivial sense that one cannot be happy unless one exists. For happiness to occur, the contents of our experience must be satisfying in some respect, and sufficiently so to outweigh whatever could make us unhappy. In their evolving continuity, the positive contents provide any happiness we can hope to amass. Those who believe in mere existence often have in mind a life that has liberated itself from the snares of worldly distractions. Rousseau meant something of the sort when he claimed to be enjoying "*le sentiment de l'existence*" after withdrawing from society in his final years. He assumed that only the simplest existence can provide a lasting happiness. This may be true, and when we discuss the nature of spirit, we shall have to reopen the issue. But even a simplified life is not the same as mere existence. That would seem to be a vacuous concept as far as happiness is concerned.

If there is reason to believe that neither play nor mere existence is a reliable guide to the character and achievement of happiness, one might decide that having a strenuous but rewarding life is preferable. Varied as their opinions have been at different times in history, many Stoic-type philosophers defended that point of view. Throughout the nineteenth century and much of the twentieth, great access to power and wealth created by modern industry encouraged people in all regions of the globe to expend enormous amounts of energy in the pursuit of diverse goals. For the most part, these enterprises were designed to eventuate in personal happiness; they were not merely economic or political. They frequently involved moral commitment and religious dedication, as suggested by the phrase "muscular Christianity."

Throwing oneself into vigorous activities has often been advised as a cure for unhappiness or spiritual malaise. In his autobiographical writings, the novelist Theodore Dreiser reports that when he was suffering from adolescent apathy his older brother sent him off to a camp in the wilderness devoted to physical labor. The tactic worked in his case. Many young men have joined the army or gone to sea in the hope that the challenges thrust upon them would not only elicit their manliness but also teach them how to live a happier life. That can sometimes occur.

At this point we may return to the book by Konrad Lorenz mentioned in Chapter 2. As I remarked, Lorenz believes that human behavior is determined by an evolutionary program that operates through a "pleasure-unpleasurable experience principle." He suggests that patterns of behavior are formed by compensating the organism with pleasures that can be obtained only by enduring some kind of unpleasurable experience. Human beings regularly undergo dangers and sufferings to which they would not have exposed themselves without the lure of a pleasurable outcome that may possibly reward their efforts. Lorenz goes on to argue that when civilized societies in the past became too successful in avoiding unpleasurable situations, the result was generally deleterious to the entire community.

According to Lorenz, this has begun to happen in the contemporary world. Technology has advanced so far that it provides most of the goods and services, comforts and luxuries that people have always wanted, and many that they could never have imagined. These benefits are often available to us with virtually no effort at all. We need only press a button or give a command in order to get consummations that formerly required lengthy, and usually tiresome, labor. The entropy of feeling that has resulted undermines the healthy and adaptive structure of the pleasure-unpleasurable experience mechanism. Having become increasingly intolerant of the necessity for unpleasurable action, people in the advanced societies shun the hard work that used to promise eventual pleasure. They therefore lose out on happiness that comes from overcoming material (and moral) difficulties. As a consequence, nothing seems to be worth struggling for, and the reliance upon instant gratification makes joyful experience impossible. "Pleasure may be achieved without paying the price of strenuous effort, but joy cannot. . . . In short, intolerance of unpleasurable experience creates deadly boredom."[7]

Lorenz thinks this entropy of feeling underlies the contemporary fear of getting involved in a love relationship as well as the increasing rate of suicide in the modern world: both are related to our pervasive sense of meaninglessness. As a possible remedy, he turns to natural challenges that a person may be willing to accept as unpleasurable necessities that can nevertheless lead to joyful resolutions. He refers to young men being cured of their boredom by being made lifeguards, or being similarly placed in dangerous circumstances. Since the human species will always be threatened by conditions that jeopardize its survival, Lorenz believes that the problem for therapy or education consists in stimulating whatever enthusiasm is required for people to undergo hardships that benefit humanity or themselves. They can find happiness in the surmounting of unavoidable obstacles, but they must be motivated to make the effort.

Much of what Lorenz says seems quite convincing. His analysis serves to prove that a quest for happiness through instant gratification may be inherently self-defeating. In recent years we have seen a massive cultivation of behavior, as in aerobic exercising and long-distance running, that yields unpleasure and even pain to favored individuals who no longer have to struggle to get routine comfort and convenience that technology now provides. Sports such as mountain climbing have long existed as the means of activating the programmed mechanism to which Lorenz refers. We could say the same about pursuits that overcome artistic or spiritual, rather than purely physical, obstacles. These all have their own intrinsic hurdles. Someday people who can satisfy their organic needs with very little effort, thanks to the wonders of future technology, may find widespread happiness mainly through these varied types of artificial endeavor.

That utopian dream was common in the United States during halcyon decades such as the 1950s. It is less prevalent nowadays. It makes sense only if we recognize that easy access to pleasure may give us much of what we want in life but not the happiness that we really crave. Bertrand Russell makes a related point. He argues that "the mere absence of effort" results not only in a lessening of enjoyment but also in the fostering of a pessimistic attitude toward one's own desires. "The man who acquires easily things for which he feels only a very moderate desire concludes that the attainment of desire does not bring happiness."[8]

As a solution to this problem, Russell suggests that we organize our lives in such a way that some of the things we want remain always unobtained. He calls this "an indispensable part of happiness."[9] At least one philosopher has criticized Russell's idea as illogical. How can we be happy, Anthony Kenny asks, as long as we are not getting what we want? I think the answer is that we acquire the ability in the present to imagine future possibilities, and this enjoyable act of imagination, together with the pleasure of having something worth seeking, compensates us for the deferred satisfactions. Even if Russell's statement were formally inconsistent, however, we could agree with him that getting everything one desires at any time eliminates appetitive and exploratory behavior that often produces its own sense of vitality and enjoyment.[10]

Similar reasoning applies to questions about the amount of effort that is optimal for ensnaring pleasures. When the instrumental struggle becomes overly burdensome, the entire enterprise may turn into misery. But where success occurs too quickly, we lose not only the goodness of pursuing it but also an authentic sense of our own reality as creatures programmed to act in order to survive. Though we would all like to win the lottery, a person to whom this happened every day would no longer feel that his or her good fortune is life-enhancing. Dreams of magical success are exhilarating only when they appear as a recognized contrast to the world we ordinarily experience. Even in children's cartoons, where almost anything is possible, the need to recognize that some forces in nature are unconquerable is preserved as a reminder of how things really are.

If we had to choose between succeeding at once in everything we care about (assuming we even understand what that means) and remaining in a state in which something to be achieved always beckons, most people would choose the latter. A paradise of spontaneous gratification without any striving for it would be no paradise at all. Though they depict unending bliss, the common fantasies about life after death mean little to us precisely because they cannot give plausible clues about what we will be doing in order to experience this glorious consummation. It is not enough to play a harp or sing hosanna forevermore, or to luxuriate in Turkish delights. Happiness requires the wanting of something for which we must make an appropriate effort. Even the heavenly host will have to tune their instruments and vocalize from time to time.

In emphasizing that happiness depends on activity rather than facile or passive enjoyment, Russell sometimes suggests that this must happen within the context of a grand and comprehensive purpose in life. In one place he states that "happiness, if it is to have any depth and solidity, demands a life built round some central purpose of a kind demanding continuous activity and permitting of progressively increasing success."[11] The idea about needing to increase one's level of success seems valid. We always run the risk of feeling bored with achievements that have reached a limit instead of continuing to augment. For many people this typically human impulse toward ever greater accomplishment matters very much. But to say that we need to have a "central" purpose that demands ceaseless action is unrealistic and much too stringent. Although some persons do find happiness in dedication to a cause or overarching goal, that cannot be a necessary condition for everyone. We may even wonder whether Russell's model specifies the *greatest* happiness. Men and women who have a consuming mission, as he advocates for all of us, must often deprive themselves of many enjoyments that contribute to a happy life. There are different types of happiness, as there are different types of aspirations, and the one that Russell recommends is not inherently better than all the others.

In opposition to my approach as well as Russell's, one might argue that by its very nature purposiveness defeats the conditions necessary for happiness. For instance, John Wisdom claims that the purposive life must always seek to attain desired goals as quickly and as easily as possible. But happiness, he insists, can only result from nonpurposive dalliance—as in sports or the having of aesthetic experience. If the goal of a journey is to reach the journey's end as directly as we can, which characterizes purposiveness in general according to Wisdom, we lose out on all the incidental pleasures that conduce to happiness and make life worth living.

I think Wisdom misconstrues both purposiveness and the nature of consummatory experience. The latter often consists in the gratifying completion of relevant purposes, and sometimes *because* they are quickly and easily completed. Moreover, goal orientation is not unique in seeking facile pleasures (which it may often eschew). The same is true of play, sport, aesthetic experience, or for that matter the enjoying of mere existence.[12]

In offering these reflections, I have assumed that happiness—and meaning as well—requires an attunement to the rational, the animal, and the vegetative aspects of our being. All three have a role in the good life. How they participate in it is still to be shown.

As a preliminary to that part of the discussion, I return to some panoramic statements about happiness that Russell makes. In one passage he remarks that happiness "depends partly upon external circumstances and partly upon oneself." He then adds: "Certain things are indispensable to the happiness of most men, but these are simple things: food and shelter, health, love, successful work, and the respect of one's own herd. To some people parenthood is also essential. Where these things are lacking, only the exceptional man can achieve happiness."[13] Elsewhere he says, as if in answer to Schopenhauer: "The secret of happiness is to face the fact that the world is horrible, horrible, *horrible.* . . . You must feel it deeply, and not brush it aside . . . and then you can start being happy again."[14]

Russell's references to love and successful work as two of the "simple things" that are indispensable for the happiness of most people is reminiscent of Freud's idea that only love and work can make us happy. In another place Russell states that the good life is "inspired by love and guided by knowledge."[15] Many writers have argued that love is "the promise of happiness," to use Stendhal's words, but that it scarcely delivers on this promise. Stendhal himself did not accept that conclusion. He thought that, regardless of how delusory love may be, it is the principal means by which happiness can be secured by human beings. He believed that nature has fashioned us that way, and that by living in accordance with nature we experience positive and authentic joy. What it means to live with nature we must next consider.

LIVING IN NATURE

❧

Throughout this book, and indeed throughout my writing as a whole, I have presupposed a "naturalist" perspective. It has always seemed intuitively right to me. Unlike some naturalists in philosophy, however, I am willing to admit that my point of view is non-verifiable. In that respect it may be considered just as metaphysical as the religious or nonnaturalistic doctrines that have predominated in traditional philosophy. In each case the philosophical imagination constructs an ultimate platform upon which it may support further arguments and inferences that constitute a coherent vision of the world. Like-minded thinkers may assume that no perspective other than theirs is wholly rational, but they are like-minded in the first place only because they share feelings and affective dispositions that are themselves deeper than (or at least prior to) whatever reasoning issues from them.

As with all labels, the term *naturalism* is just a signpost that solves no problems in itself but rather alerts us to difficulties, as well as insights, that are indigenous to it. At this moment in the history of ideas, we may find widespread agreement in rejecting the anti-naturalistic attitude of ascetics of the Middle Ages. Contemporary men and women have little sympathy with would-be saints who think they get nearer to reality by mortifying the flesh and sacrificing all possible earthly happiness. We tend to consider such people pathological: far from having escaped the bounds of nature, they would seem to illustrate the hurtful consequences of neglecting them. But though we may denigrate the ascetic mentality, we delude ourselves if we think that the idea of accepting nature and living in accordance with it is self-evidently right, or even capable of eliciting general agreement.

To clarify our thinking about the natural, we should study John Stuart Mill's essay entitled "Nature." In it Mill seeks to refute those philosophers who think that living the good life means acting "naturally" or "in conformity with" the dictates of nature. If by the term *nature* we mean whatever happens in the world apart from human intervention, Mill argues, the good life must always consist in changing and improving nature rather than complying with it. He claims that if we duplicate the ways of nature or act in accordance with them, we perpetuate the suffering and the destructiveness that characterize all natural events. Those who are cruel or evil do what comes naturally, given what nature is. Those who are virtuous and those who attain happiness have learned how to alter it, redirecting it toward moral and aesthetic ends that human beings systematically impose.

Throughout his argument, Mill insists that philosophers are mistaken when they encourage people to "imitate" nature, to take it as a "model" for justifiable conduct, to make it "a test of right and wrong, good and evil," to "obey" it, to behave in "conformity to" it, to "follow" it, or to "live in accordance with" it. I have put quotation marks around these words because they are all terms that Mill uses, not indiscriminately or as if they were synonymous, but with very little attempt to show the differences among them. Yet the diversity within their various connotations seems to me highly relevant.

We may well agree with Mill that we often need to overcome nature rather than remaining obedient to it. As he also says, humanity triumphs over nature when bridges are built to join shores that natural events had originally separated. Mill does well to assert that agencies of nature frequently confront man as "enemies, from whom he must wrest, by force and ingenuity, what little he can for his own use."[1] To the extent that civilization and human artifice of any sort conquer perilous forces in nature, it is thwarted, not obeyed—and properly so on many occasions.

Mill may therefore be right in saying that by and large nature ought not to be imitated. So much of nature consists in ruthless killing and senseless destruction that we have no reason to use it as an overall model of desirable action by human beings. Marauding criminals who feel little compunction about attacking an innocent victim in order to get something worth having may feel that they are imitating some law of nature that operates in them as it does throughout the universe. To encourage such people to use nature as their guide, as many Romantics of the nineteenth century did, can result in strengthening selfish and immoral tendencies that society should make every effort to eradicate.

Although Mill's point is well taken to this extent, the rest of what he says about nature and our possible attitudes toward it may not be equally tenable. It is one thing to doubt that humankind should imitate nature or indiscriminately employ it as a blueprint; it is something else, and very different, to deny the advisability of living in accordance with nature. Mill makes the latter assertion in claiming that "the duty of man is the same in respect to his own nature as in respect to the nature of all other things, namely not to follow but to amend it."[2] If Mill is correct, however, even "the duty of man" would have to arise from some artificial or nonnatural aspect of our being.

For deontologists such as Kant, that might be a suitable assumption. But it is one that Mill can hardly make, since the utilitarian ethics that he most famously promotes explicitly predicates an ultimate foundation for morality in the desires, the feelings, the inclinations of human beings. Formulating his ethical standard in this fashion, Mill never intimates that our condition as appetitive and purposive creatures can be amended. On the contrary, he accepts this state as a given, a prior fact of nature that determines what will constitute a reasonable and defensible system of morality.

Is Mill's philosophy basically confused? His remarks are puzzling, and the language he uses in various places is ambiguous; but even so, we should continue to seek a reading of his text that will reveal some logical coherence and residual insight. For instance, when he addresses himself to the question of whether reason should show "deference" to instinct, as maintained by various philosophers who tell us to live in accordance with nature, Mill consistently argues that the instinctive element of human nature is not the part that manifests our capacity for goodness or wisdom. He sees the latter as issuing from "a long course of artificial education" that renders habitual whatever humanitarian sentiments may occur and lend themselves to cultivation. Apart from the restraints that society carefully enforces, there would seem to be hardly any redeeming qualities that belong to what Mill calls "the untutored feelings of human nature." [3]

Mill does recognize that what is admirable in humanity must have some instinctual source. But he considers this benign potentiality meager as compared with the vicious and undesirable bulk of what is natural to our species. Almost everything that is good or right or worthy of preservation he ascribes to artificial nurturing of the very small amount of instinct that is actually humane and ethical. The rest, he believes, must be severely curtailed or even extirpated.

In saying this, Mill has in mind a specific conception of what is good and morally justifiable. It is enunciated in his work entitled *Utilitarianism*. But there he presents a different picture of what is or is not "natural" in human nature. Probing for an "ultimate sanction" as the foundation of utilitarian morality, Mill distinguishes between sanctions that are external and those that are internal. The former involve fear of punishment, and hope for rewards, that persons or institutions instill in those who are subject to their control. Mill perceives that this alone cannot constitute an ultimate sanction for morality. That issues from what he calls "the social feelings of mankind; the desire to be in unity with our fellow creatures." [4]

Mill speaks of this internal sanction as "a powerful principle in human nature," and he maintains: "The social state is at once so natural, so necessary, and so habitual to man, that except in some unusual circumstances or by an effort of voluntary abstraction, he never conceives himself otherwise than as a member of a body." [5] Mill then shows how life in society leads people to identify their feelings with what is good for others in that society. "The good of others becomes . . . a thing naturally and necessarily to be attended to, like any of the physical conditions of our existence."[6] This feeling is nourished by what Mill calls "the contagion of sympathy and the influences of education." He states that "a complete web of corroborative association is woven round it, by the powerful agency of the external sanctions. This mode of conceiving ourselves and human life, as civilization goes on, is felt to be more and more natural."[7]

It will be noted that Mill refers only to what is "felt" as natural. In order for that feeling to be itself a "powerful natural sentiment," as Mill says when he claims to have found in it an ultimate sanction for morality, it would have to be innate and possibly inescapable in human nature. But unlike Hume, Mill explicitly denies that sympathy or fellow feeling is innate in human beings. "This feeling in most individuals," he remarks, "is much inferior in strength to their selfish feelings, and is often wanting altogether." To this he adds: "But to those who have it, it possesses all the characters of a natural feeling."[8]

Formulating his ideas about social feeling in this way, Mill undermines his suggestion that utilitarianism can be justified by reference to what is inherently natural. If the majority of human beings have selfish feelings that are greater and much stronger than their social feelings, a desire to maximize happiness along utilitarian lines cannot be deemed a powerful natural sentiment. It cannot serve as an ultimate sanction of the sort that Mill is looking for. If social feeling has a natural aura only among some people in certain segments of civilization at a particular stage of development, the most that Mill can be said to have established is the fact that it operates sporadically among human beings. Those who do not have this feeling innately may conclude that, aside from the external sanctions imposed by others, nothing requires them to cultivate it in themselves.

This difficulty recurs pervasively in Mill's moral theory. Having cited the social feelings as an ultimate sanction, he advocates that they be buttressed and extended beyond one's own society and to the benefit of humanity as a whole. Though humanitarian feelings begin as "germs" that need to be fostered, he hopes that each generation will progressively encourage their further sprouting through education as well as legislation. Mill is thus favoring compliance with the part of nature that resists individual selfishness. If, however, selfishness is as strong and frequent as he himself believes, what justifies our giving special importance to fellow feeling? Why should we want to live in accordance with this minor aspect of human nature? To recommend his utilitarian standard, Mill must offer conclusive reasons for overcoming the wholly selfish attitudes he considers characteristic of our species. But what are these reasons? And how do they provide a secure foundation for his or anyone else's naturalistic ethics?

※

Mill might reply that in the essay "Nature" he mainly wished to deny there are grounds for following nature in its entirety (what he sometimes calls "the course of nature"). As opposed to idealists and most Romantic theorists, he wanted to prove we live a good life not by imitating the general pattern of nature but rather by acting in accordance with the few elements of it that are truly commendable. In *Utilitarianism* he explicates what is "commendable" in a way that I have not yet mentioned. This analysis occurs in his remarks about quality versus quantity of pleasure. Having identified happiness with pleasure, Mill goes on to argue that some kinds of pleasure are "more desirable and more valuable than others."[9] Between two pleasures, if one is qualitatively much superior to the other, that one is more desirable and more conducive to happiness even if it provides a lesser quantity of pleasure or even a greater amount of discontent. Mill's conception of nature as related to morality appears in the reasons he gives for preferring quality over quantity.

He begins by asserting that the only competent judges in this matter are people who have had experience of both types of pleasure. He then insists that such persons would unquestionably choose the kind that is recognized to be qualitatively higher:

Few human creatures would consent to be changed into any of the lower animals, for a promise of the fullest allowance of a beast's pleasures; no intelligent human being would consent to be a fool, no instructed person would be an ignoramus, no person of feeling and conscience would be selfish and base, even though they should be persuaded that the fool, the dunce, or the rascal is better satisfied with his lot than they are with theirs.[10]

To account for the making of such choices, Mill explores different attitudes that have sometimes been adduced by moralists—pride, the love of liberty and personal independence, the love of power, the love of excitement. He finally settles on "a sense of dignity" as something every human being possesses, occurring most prominently in men and women who cultivate their "higher faculties." So essential is this sense of dignity to the happiness of these people that they would reject any alternative life, even one that yields greater pleasure and less discontent. It is in this context that Mill says that it is "better to be a human being dissatisfied than a pig satisfied; better to be Socrates dissatisfied than a fool satisfied."[11]

Mill's entire line of thought presupposes that there is something natural, and uniquely human, in preferring the so-called higher pleasures and acting out of a sense of dignity. He relies on more than the obvious fact that the human race has powers of intellect and imagination that set it apart from other species. He claims such differences eventuate in pleasures that will be acknowledged as better by most or all persons who have experienced them. That is what gives these pleasures their qualitative advantage and makes them definitive of human happiness at its best. If fools or pigs choose a foolish or a piggish way of life, Mill says, it is because they know only one of the possibilities, while the competent judges who decide that other pleasures are superior know both. But why is this greater knowledge (assuming the judges have it) crucial as far as valuation is concerned? The relative goodness of alternate pleasures must be determined by individual preferences, and in the case of the judges Mill envisages these preferences will derive from the sense of dignity that matters so much to them. Unless human nature ordains or guarantees the supreme importance Mill ascribes to this sense of dignity, his argument cannot be persuasive for those who have a different sensibility.

❋

Mill's utilitarianism is often said to deviate radically from the ethical theory he inherited from his father and from Bentham. Certainly this is true inasmuch as Mill links the nature of happiness to the quality of pleasures and therefore denies that happiness is a function of quantity alone. But of further significance, I think, is Mill's emphasis upon dignity as the basis of the higher pleasures that constitute what he calls the greatest happiness for human beings. Not only is the sense of dignity an ultimate in his ethical analysis, which makes us wonder whether he is still a hedonist, but also he treats it as that which reveals what lies deepest in our nature.

Whether or not he thinks we have an "instinct" for dignity, Mill regards it as a human reality that lies at the core of our moral being. If it were a minor or occasional phenomenon, as he claims that sympathy is apart from social conditioning, it could not sustain the qualitative criteria for evaluation that he finds paramount. Whatever Mill says about the need to overcome nature rather than modeling one's behavior on it, he must be interpreted as meaning that a good and happy life for human beings consists in conformity to that much of nature which manifests itself as our innate sense of dignity.

I will not attempt to resolve the intricate paradoxes in Mill's utilitarian philosophy. On the one hand, he advocates acceptance of nature insofar as he makes happiness his ethical standard and defines happiness in terms of pleasure. On the other hand, his belief that the sense of dignity is basic to authoritative judgments about the most desirable kind of happiness implies a more circumscribed, but more problematic, attitude toward what is natural. Acting in accordance with an innate sense of dignity can always throttle impulses and inclinations that also come from nature—for instance, desires that propel us toward swinish pleasures of the body. Dignity implies awareness of social expectations, an appearance of decorum in the eyes of others, and even a sense of righteousness. This pole in Mill's theory brings him closer to Kant than he himself may have realized.

It also alerts us to aspects of the Kantian philosophy that are worth examining in this context.

Kant thinks of morality as an a priori and therefore nonnatural restraint upon happiness. If we follow our natural bent, Kant argues, we may possibly attain whatever happiness is available to us as human beings. But on his view, this alone cannot constitute the good life. That involves ethical rectitude, which he explains in terms of transcendental reason and self-legislation by the will. The ideal would consist in a harmonization between inclination and reason, happiness and virtue, but Kant denies the likelihood of that ever occurring on earth. If we give morality greatest importance in our lives, as he insists all rational creatures must, we are constrained to limit or even sacrifice our desire to find happiness by living in accordance with nature. While agreeing with those who claim that happiness results from conformity to the natural, Kant insists that morality takes precedence and often negates this goodness for which we all hunger.

From Mill's point of view, Kant's philosophy is mistaken in two respects: it identifies the basis of morality with reason rather than social feeling; and it naively assumes that authentic happiness comes from doing what comes naturally. Mill's emphasis upon dignity and the "higher" pleasures may have served as a bridge toward the Kantian view of life, as I have been suggesting, but Mill wished to establish a radically different conception of morality, one that defines itself in terms of happiness while also showing that the preferred kind of happiness to which human beings have access entails a major overcoming of nature rather than submission to it.

In the discussion that follows in this book I will develop a view that differs from both Kant's and Mill's. Mill was following in the tradition of Hume and others in the eighteenth century who saw ethics not as a metaphysical mandate but as an offshoot of humanitarian sentiments, and that seems to me the right approach to any possible morality. At the same time, however, I share Kant's intuitive belief that every form of happiness depends on our ability to live in accordance with nature. But how are we to understand, and properly interpret, this ability? If we can make sense of it, we may be able to detect the outlines of a moral theory that goes beyond Kant as well as Mill.

In working toward that end, we should return to the remarks I made in suggesting that Schopenhauer's pessimism bespeaks a lack of faith in nature. To establish the mere possibility of happiness, I referred to the goodness that animate creatures, including human beings, feel when they accept the vegetative element in their natural state and thereby enjoy whatever consummations it provides under favorable conditions. But no active animal can live at the vegetative level only, though comatose individuals may be thought to approximate it. In any event, human happiness necessarily involves more than just the vegetative, and therefore we would consider it odd if someone said that a man or woman in a coma is enjoying a happy life. Under normal circumstances unconsciousness is not only an interlude between periods of alertness but also a recharging of energies that the organism will soon be using overtly. These kinetic forces are requisite for something to be an animal and to have an intellect. Only in that context is human happiness possible.

The animal powers to which I refer are evident in everything organisms do explicitly as a means of adapting to the surrounding world, and in their conscious attempt to profit from it. We speak of creatures like ourselves "struggling" with the environment, as if to master and prevail upon it. The goods of life must generally be torn from their natural integument. Only rarely are they bestowed without some effort on our part. From an early age all animals learn that they must take action, out of their own center and most often selfishly, if they wish to survive and to flourish. They are quickly habituated to the needs and desires with which they identify their particular mode of existence. They become accustomed to any self-sustaining behavior that tends to satisfy their inclinations. And since they themselves initiate this behavior and carry it to fulfillment (if they can), they may feel that they are free and independent of the nature they seek to dominate. In an obvious sense they are, but unless nature supported them throughout the process, they would be completely helpless. Nature gives them the capacity to succeed in this endeavor as well as the motivation to try to do so. Without faith in the availability of nature for this purpose, no one would ever think that what he or she does in the world, and to the world, can make any vital difference.

In describing this mode of living in nature, I borrow and adapt Santayana's term "animal faith." He had in mind the fact that all animals, even skeptical philosophers, instinctively surmount epistemological doubts induced in them by reason and experience. This happens because life itself requires faith in the existence and irrefutable presence of the external world. Hume had said something similar when he remarked that he cannot live in the ordinary way that everyone does as long as he attends to the abstract implications of his own analyses. His epistemological skepticism does, and must, fall away once he joins the company of his friends and plays a game of whist. For then he reverts to organic structures in himself that precede and that make possible his technical interests as a philosopher.

My conception of animal faith incorporates much of what Hume and Santayana meant, but also I wish to emphasize the non-epistemological dimensions of this response. Action in the midst of nature shows forth what it is to be an animal of the sort that we happen to be. Animal faith is an affirming of oneself as just the animal one is. It functions in varying degrees as a lubricant in the process of taking and accepting whatever manifests one's animality. This faith in one's nature appears most graphically in the behavior of a dominant baboon striding through his troop with absolute assurance about his personal supremacy. In its focused mien, in its projection of physical strength and unmatchable power, the baboon radiates self-confidence that I have also seen in human beings in a similar social setting. The grandiose display may only be a theatrical performance that some individuals cultivate and perfect as a means of enjoying desired privileges. But, as with actors on a stage, the accomplished presentation of a self-asserting self is a notable achievement. Behavior of this sort, whether in a dominant baboon or an impressive human being, may be socially justifiable inasmuch as it reassures the other members of the group that someone is in charge and apparently capable of leading them all.

The man or woman who lives in nature, who lives in conformity to it, has the kind of animal faith we observe in dominant baboons even when it shows itself in acts that are not similar to theirs. In different species animal faith resorts to different types of behavior. Although baboon society is organized on the lines of a military dictatorship, the social order of chimpanzees is often just the opposite, given to anarchy rather than regimentation. In our species, the leaders sometimes attain their dominance by serving as "first among equals." But whether or not we aspire to be first in this political sense, and regardless of our resemblance to either baboons or chimpanzees, we live in accordance with our animal nature to the extent that the goodness, the suitability, the preestablished rightness in being the animal that we are appears in anything we do to stay alive. All animals must act for their own survival, but only those that do so with love for themselves as animals can be said to live in accordance with their nature. Living with animal faith means having the requisite self-love.

Animal faith seems to occur more overtly—more "naturally," as we say—among creatures that we human beings call animals. We are often ashamed of our bodily functions in a way that they are not. There is at least an iota of puritanism in everyone who is human. Unless animals have been domesticated and thus exposed to psychological problems that are native to ourselves, they are free of most of the inhibitions that make human nature so unnatural. I often marvel at the self-assurance that members of other species have, even those that must scurry to find food and to avoid being eaten themselves. Their instincts hedge and restrain them as much as, often more than, civilization does with us. Yet they seem less preoccupied and perturbed about their creaturely condition than is the case with even primitive people.

As human beings, we blandly assume that lack of intellect makes these other life forms different in this respect. And to some extent that must be true. At the same time, however, we know that non-human animals frequently have greater memory than we do, and greater perceptual power in various modalities. Moreover, their intelligence is usually quite adequate for their particular needs. The conceptual strength that is distinctive of our species would be a useless burden for many others, an encumbrance that could only interfere with their normal lifestyles without necessarily augmenting their ability to survive. If animal faith is less evident among us in comparison to them, it may be that we are endowed with an excess of intellect. Shakespeare's *Hamlet* is a testament to this as a possible explanation of human sorrow.

Intellect is inherently the ability to solve problems by means that are often novel and unforeseeable in advance. With it as our natural resource we have been able to conquer all other animals on this planet. So versatile is this tool that it can even turn inward and study itself. Once it does that, it may use its problem-solving competence to speculate about methods of surmounting its own tendency to undermine animal faith. These methods range within a wide spectrum of responsiveness. The solution at one extreme may involve a radical cessation of reason, induced by drugs perhaps or by reigning ideologies that minimize the importance of intellect as a human faculty. But given what it is to be our type of organism, this is always hazardous. For one thing, it puts us at the mercy of hostile forces in the environment as well as enemies who can use their greater or more effective intellect to destroy us.

The solution at the opposite extreme is fraught with equal danger. It involves the attempt to accept one's cognitive being so completely and unflinchingly that one no longer minds sacrificing the gratification and emotional sustenance that come from satisfying the needs of our body. Philosophers since Plato, and earlier among the pre-Socratics, have often sought a utopian condition in which all human issues could be dealt with in terms of coordinates geared to intellect alone. People who have had little of it themselves glibly talk about "the life of the mind." But in itself the mind has no life. It is always embedded in the life that nature has given us through the body, and that includes much that is not at all mental. For relatively short periods, and within artificial bounds that may sometimes be helpful, even essential for some beneficial purpose, the mind can operate on its own, similar to a computer that has been unplugged but runs for a while on the energy stored in its battery. Eventually the cognitive equipment must be recharged through fulfillments that belong to our animal and vegetative incarnation.

A compromise between the two extremes is clearly optimal. And as with most conceptual compromises, the agency for the desired harmonization is imagination directed toward some ideal. This employment of imagination is fundamental in the kind of faith I am trying to describe. Those who feel the goodness of using their intellect to the fullest, whether in science, mathematics, or the various arts, are able to succeed because they have access to whatever imagination is requisite for the task at hand. If they have a sense of confidence and of mastery in what they do, it is because they are empowered by natural forces attuned to just those imaginative procedures that intellect needs in order to do its work.

These procedures are generally envisaged as imagined possibilities relevant to some ideal that is pertinent to the enterprise. For that reason alone, we must understand the nature of idealization as well as imagination if we are to construct a viable theory about faith in nature and the human capacity to live in conformity to it. When we act in accordance with our nature as intellectual beings, we have faith in our ability to solve problems that reality forces upon us and that our imagination helps us to confront creatively in the service of whatever ideal we care about. This is an aspect of faith that is not at all reducible to faith in ourselves as either vegetative or animal entities. Each defines its own attitude toward life.

In principle there is no necessary conflict between vegetative, animal, and cognitive modes of faith. In different societies and at different moments in a person's life, competition among them may be intense, sometimes causing disunity and even civil war. But that itself becomes a problem that intellect may address in cooperation with imagination and idealization. We therefore need to analyze these elements of our nature in greater detail. This will bring us closer to formulating a comprehensive theory about the meaning and the happiness that living in nature can provide. That, in turn, may reveal how a desirable harmonization of nature and spirit can possibly occur.

6

IMAGINATION
& IDEALIZATION

❧

Though imagination and idealization are pervasive as human realities, art—like love—reveals their great importance in the search for happiness as well as meaning, and in relation to nature as well as spirit. For many persons nowadays the love of art has become a religion. The orthodox faiths were generally afraid that this might happen. They suspected that artistic imagination working in combination with the idealization of values that ordinary people cherish might eventually displace the spiritual as well as the natural benefits that religion has always promised. The churches learned, early in their history, how to tame and co-opt music, literature, and painting, but they remained suspicious of artistic expressiveness. A graven image could lead the unwary to confuse nature and spirit, to treat things that are alluring through the senses as if their charm, their beauty, their holiness as consummations came directly from themselves. The artist had to be domesticated, like a cat or dog that lacks the higher rationality and metaphysical awareness that human beings have regularly considered the justification for their dominant creeds.

This tactic worked for many centuries. Art was either banished from the spiritual aspects of life, or else scrutinized and censored by ecclesiastical powers that kept it on a leash. Art nevertheless performed a useful function that all the religions have recognized and approved: it awakened the imagination of even the most reluctant parishioners, directing it toward whatever ideals the authorities wished to promote.

Discussing imagination and the making of ideals in previous books, I have emphasized their ability to create meaning in the lives of human beings. But there are questions we must ask about such creativity. Does it bespeak a talent for enlarging reality that only certain people have—specifically men and women we call "artists"? Or is the creative capacity something present in us all, and therefore an element in any viable conception of what reality must be, or at least appears to be, for our kind of creature?

This dilemma may have confronted even prehistoric cave dwellers who marveled at drawings of sacred animals that some local painter sketched on the walls of their communal home. Whether the artist was himself a priest or only a chosen hand transmitting the animistic views of an inspired shaman, his fellows must have stood in awe at his ability to evoke the spirit of the bull or bison they had slain and now wished to placate. It might never have occurred to these simple men and women that they themselves were undergoing a creative act merely in seeing the two-dimensional figure as more than just a beast in nature, more than just a brutish thing with no spiritual import of any sort. Yet the artist would have been only a doodler, and might never have undertaken the enterprise at all, unless he could rely on their imaginative interpretation of his drawings. The shaman, or whoever commissioned this work, was himself a spokesman for the verities that constituted the recognized religion of the tribe. Its sustaining faith enveloped everyone in the group because each person participated in the unified imagination that created a meaningful life for them day by day.

If we accept this kind of explanation, we may find that our thinking about imagination, idealization, and art itself may have to be altered greatly. Our received ideas (received from preconceptions distinctive of the Western world in the last two or three hundred years) lead us to consider artists as uniquely creative individuals, as people specially endowed with God-given faculties that set them apart from the rest of humanity. Nor is this view without some basis in fact: musicians have an acuity to pitch and possibly harmonic structure that often is congenital; painters have a "feel" for lines and colors that probably precedes their training in the visual arts; dancers have a natural rhythm in their movements that most other people are not born with and can never acquire; and so on for each mode of aesthetic creativity. What makes these outstanding persons into artists, however, is their ability to innovate productively. This comes from powers of imagination that are characteristic of our species, even though few men and women realize their potentialities to the extent that successful practitioners of an art are able to.

The capacity to innovate is the most obvious attribute of imagination, but there is another that is of equal relevance. Not only does imagination present us with the spectacle (astounding in itself) of something that never was or ever will be—centaurs, gods, novel sounds, colors not seen in nature—but also it provides its free entertainment as a demonstration of what is meaningful to us and other human beings. It does not operate as a random system of invention. Imagination creates in accordance with predilections that reveal what we want and usually do not have, what we fear and cannot escape in actuality, what we care about and hope to further by clever permutations in our thought. Imagination is thus the epiphany and expression of human values, the elaboration of what has meaning as that which we find to be good or evil in some possible reality.

At the same time, it is through imagination that human beings create standards of excellence that define what they *accept* as good or evil. The ideals that govern so much of our existence are not present in nature in the way that sensations or perceptual objects are. These too may depend on imaginative processes, but not of the same sort. Idealization arises through social intercourse in a manner that is peculiar to itself. It is the principal means by which we determine what our collective and individual destiny will be. It enables us to assert our autonomy in the face of physical necessities we cannot control, and generally cannot outwit, in any other way. Without appropriate acts of imagination, however, the making of ideals could not occur. The interrelation between these two is what we must now try to decipher.

In the first volume of *The Nature of Love*, I criticized both Freud and Santayana for their use of the term *idealization*. In Freud it normally means "overvaluation of the object." In Santayana's twentieth-century variation of Neoplatonism, the word refers to the way in which persons or things that we love represent and even embody ideals that are themselves the true objects of our love. By defining idealization as just the *making* of ideals, I was able to argue for a different approach. Unlike Freud, I did not wish to assume that all love is illusory or deceptive or in general an erroneous estimation of what some thing or person is "really" worth. Unlike Santayana and the Platonists, I wanted to emphasize that love means an acceptance of that object as it is in itself, as the particularity it happens to be rather than as a representation or showing forth of an abstract ideal. In my earlier writing, and here as well, I take idealization to be human nature creating ideals by formulating and then pursuing possible perfections whose importance we ourselves bestow through varied types of imagination. Idealization can eventuate as the love of ideals, but neither the love of persons nor the love of things is reducible to that alone.

The relationship between imagination and idealization is both organic and dialectical. The creation of ideals that awaken our imaginative faculties is fundamental in our species; and yet without imagination, ideals could not exist. Throughout its functioning, imagination reveals but also enriches the ideals that matter to an individual person or society. Is there a paradox in this? Not really, since human beings are always born into a world itself replete with idealizations and the products of imagination that are already interactive among themselves. The growing child has access to both. He or she develops by accentuating the different components and by constantly modulating the contents of their interaction.

In the history of philosophy it was Romantic idealism of the early nineteenth century that first understood, or wholly appreciated, the connection between imagination and idealization. Instead of treating reason as a wondrous faculty that puts us in touch with ultimate truths not accessible through any other means, the idealists emphasized the degree to which our vision of reality inevitably depends on feats of imagination that reach beyond mere intellect. Since reason alone is deficient, the idealists concluded, human beings systematically create their idea of what the world is like. That can happen, it was thought, only through conceptual excursions within imagination. These excursions were not value free, however, since human beings were always pursuing ideals without which no one could go on living.

Much of nineteenth-century idealism was both benign and humanistic. But it was vitiated by metaphysical egotism that was residual to its general outlook. The philosophers assumed that since idealization conjoined with imagination is basic in our experience of reality it follows that reality itself must be determined by these subjectivistic phenomena. That was a non sequitur in their thinking, as recognized by all realist critics of the idealists. The realists correctly pointed out that even if imagination and idealization are crucial for understanding human nature they tell us little about the nature of *reality*: they are important as elements of psychology, not cosmology.

Most of the theoretical speculation of Freud can be seen as an extension of the realist approach. Freud studied idealization in terms of various psychological mechanisms in our nature, and he showed how artfully imagination (whose mysterious workings he sometimes traced to the unconscious) both fashioned and modified ideals in accordance with organic needs. Freud's mistake consisted in believing there must be a single, uniform system that governs the operations of imagination and idealization, and that it must always be a manifestation of libidinal energy. This idea was less egocentric than the idealist metaphysics Freud wished to replace, but it was equally dubious.

In an attempt to harmonize idealist and realist perspectives of the nineteenth and twentieth centuries, we should note that both have often assumed that everything in our experience is permeated by meaning. That was a fundamental tenet for most adherents to Romantic idealism. They considered our pervasive creation of meaning as the clearest indication of how the human mind invests the world with whatever reality it has for us. For his part, Freud concentrated on phenomena such as dreams, slips of the tongue, and seemingly trivial self-deceptions because he was convinced that they, as well as other previously neglected elements of experience, revealed that everything in consciousness has a meaning of its own.

Both Freud and the idealists may have been mistaken, as I believe they were, in thinking that there is a single pattern of meaning that pulsates in a coherent rhythm throughout our life. But they were surely right to assert that we cannot understand what appears to us as "the world" unless we recognize the created meanings that are pervasively inseparable from it.

They were also right in seeing that the meaningfulness of what we call reality always expresses our own systems of value. The constant interplay between imagination and idealization makes that inevitable. However inventive our imagination may be, it functions under self-imposed restraints that indicate that some standard or ideal is being conceived and usually sought. When El Greco, in his painting of Toledo, rearranged the location of various buildings in that city, his imaginative gesture was daring and even shocking because the title of his work made it seem that he was offering a literal representation of a fixed reality—the actual city of Toledo, which remains the same for everyone. Why did El Greco choose to upset people by presenting the view as he did? Not merely to assert the freedom of artistic imagination but also to make a statement about perception's dependence upon values. In the alembic of his visual creativity there must have been an ideal image of how the city "ought" to look.

We expect this of artists, since they are sensitive to alternative beauties that may never appear in nature. But something comparable belongs to the ordinary experience of nonartistic persons as well. In our search for meaning, we see the everyday world under the aspect of goals, values, ideals that matter to us and that calibrate and readjust whatever instruments of perception we acquire through innate physiology.

These ministering angels, the ideals that hover above the battle-field of reality and also enter into the fray, are infinitely diverse. There is no single pattern that can do justice to the plurality of meaning they create on different occasions and for different people. In fathering them forth, imagination is wholly innovative—not in the sense that it propagates them out of nothing, for the germinal forces of life are always operative in this birth of meaning out of brute materiality, but rather in the sense that each new creation is largely unforeseeable. Idealization is a variable offshoot of imagi-nation, which enables us to glimpse some desired possibility that then becomes an actuality of our aspiration. The resulting ideals require and hence elicit further acts of imagination that are needed to serve whatever idiosyncratic ends some group or individual anoints as valuable and worthy of pursuit by everyone. The ricochet of meaning that results constitutes vitality in a species such as ours.

❅

These remarks about imagination and idealization should be placed in the context of epistemological thinking that was fundamental in the work of Hume and Kant. Having analyzed the contents of the mind as either "impressions" that derive directly from our sensa-tions or else "ideas" that organize impressions into the objects of perceptual experience, Hume argued that imagination is the faculty that makes this process possible. The mind, he thought, is passive in receiving impressions but active and creative insofar as imagination orders and consolidates the incoming sensations into manifold pat-terns that then become our ideas of the external world.

In a somewhat parallel fashion, Hume suggested that ideals affecting moral and aesthetic behavior must also arise from imagi-nation. Fabricating goals that matter to us, it exceeds the limits of what perception or reason would nominate as the real world. Not only does imagination add to whatever exists as reality, but also it leads some people—notably idealist philosophers, many of whom then criticized Hume in the following century—to infer that reality is itself a product of quasi-human idealization. And to some extent, of course, Hume recognized that what they maintained is true of *our* reality. Their error consisted in assuming that truths about ourselves must yield a blueprint for what is true of everything.

This egregious aspect of idealist thought can be found in major elements of Kant's philosophy. Although his famous critique prescribes severe limits to the metaphysical capability of reason, it also accords to rationality a dignity and importance that no previous philosophy had affirmed so thoroughly. This is apparent even in Kant's distinction between the beautiful and the sublime. Both are modes of imagination. In presenting us with something we experience as beautiful, Kant says, imagination calls to mind—re*minds* us of—an object that represents the ordinary world of perception. The object fits the ideational form or pattern that defines it as what it is, whatever it may be, and imagination delights in its own free, untrammeled ability to evoke something of this sort even if none actually exists. That is why, Kant believes, beauty means so much to us. By contributing to the intuition of sublimity, however, imagination reveals a power of the human mind that is greater still. The sublime is more than just the beautiful.

Kant's view may seem odd since he maintains that the sublime extends beyond our ability to comprehend its object through any of our usual concepts or modes of perception. The vastness of the universe is sublime, he remarks, but hardly comprehensible. Our imaginative intuition strikes us with awe and the kind of aesthetic fulfillment that is afforded by vistas of huge mountains or thundering waterfalls, and yet the universe is infinitely baffling to us. Though affording us the experience of sublimity, imagination finds itself unable to fit its object into the mold of any formal pattern that we can fathom. On the contrary, Kant asserts, the sublime affects us as that which can*not* be comprehended by human faculties. Yet its object is discernible through reason, and therefore imagination must be relying upon a superlative capacity of our rational faculty.

Kant concludes that in the experience of sublimity, the human spirit is defeated, and therefore imagination cannot provide anything like the pleasure that beauty yields. But since the sublime depends on ideas summoned forth through reason alone, we glory in having a mentality that is masterful enough to feed our imagination in this manner. Regardless of its ultimate failure, reason succeeds merely by making its heroic attempt and showing itself to best advantage.

As another way of articulating Kant's distinction, we can say that through beauty imagination gives us pleasurable feelings of appreciating the nature of objectification, but through the sublime it reveals how marvelous our rational faculty is despite its inability to comprehend an object whose grandeur it nevertheless evokes. The awesome respect we feel is directed toward ideas of reason, whose contents may elude our attempts to understand them but nevertheless create a sense of our own grandeur as creatures who can have such ranging conceptions at all.

We can easily see why this theory about the sublime and its glorification of reason through imagination was so attractive to nineteenth-century idealists (Schelling, for instance). Although I am revolted by Schelling's eagerness to puff up the human mind, whose rational faculty he extols extravagantly not for having understood the universe but only for having tried to do so, I, too, recognize the virtue in distinguishing this use of imagination from the kind that underlies our experience of beauty. I have previously voiced my doubts about notions of absolute nothingness as a metaphysical category, and in fact I have denied that they can be rendered comprehensible. But I also admitted that they have some bizarre and irresistible meaning for me, affecting my feelings and lingering in a hazy fringe of my awareness, like a forgotten name or face that keeps escaping consciousness. I think it is this kind of experience to which the idealists were referring. They call our attention to an indeterminate reach of imagination that cultivates deep and often troublesome intuitions about some ultimate reality. To think that these justify, or even support, an ontology of absolute Being is, however, inadmissible.

Whether we define the sublime in terms of the infinity of the universe or some underlying nothingness, the fact remains that such language makes sense only as an extrapolation beyond ordinary discourse. It expresses inchoate feelings arising from our mere existence as human beings but implicates no ideas of pure reason.

The mind works metaphorically, through extensions of empirical understanding wrenched beyond its usual employment by some philosopher's imagination. The sense of sublimity is audacious in its ideational thrust and tantalizing in its suggestiveness, but scarcely worthy of being taken as proof that mental processes can be projected upon the universe in the way that either Kant or the idealists claimed.

The experience of the sublime, and its relation to reality, must therefore be explained differently. Our feelings about the universe, either as infinite or as absolutely nothing, may even preclude its possible sublimity. The sentiment of awe is a variant of fear. Our heart sinks when we imagine ourselves as tiny, insignificant droplets in the cosmic flow, and if we think that nothingness is at the base of everything, we are more likely to be depressed than uplifted. To find the additional ingredient needed for us to have a sense of anything as sublime, we must turn to the human propensity for idealization. Without it, imagination could not engender the requisite feeling.

Whether we are gazing at a sunset that takes our breath away, or the splendor of the aurora borealis, or for that matter any glittering display of stars scattered across the sky on a cloudless night, we experience the sublime under the aspect of various ideals that have aesthetic and moral validity for us. The scene appears sublime only if we feel confident that all is well in the universe, that some ideal and finely ordered intention has prearranged the grand spectacle we are observing, that the scene betokens a humane or quasi-artistic design, a cosmic equivalent to the purposive beauty and aesthetic goodness that we encounter in works of art.

To this extent the sublime, whether in natural landscape or in our conception of reality itself, overlaps with the beautiful and may even be considered a subset of it. It is the part of beauty that deals with raging storms or plunging cascades or the astounding panoply of galaxies that populate the cosmos. If we have no faith in the beneficent beauty of the universe as a whole, it will have no sublimity for us.

It may nevertheless occasion a sense of wonder—as when we contemplate the big bang, the expansion of known existence out of a subatomic particle, and the possibility that in the future all this may reverse itself. Such wonderment is not the same as sublimity. Charged as it is with confusion or simple terror, our wonder can leave us speechless and incapable of learning how we should behave. That was the response of Job when the Voice Out of the Whirlwind overwhelmed him with its proof of his unimportance in the face of its stupendous power. Job did not experience the sublime, just the horror of his human worthlessness. Awe and the sense of wonder yield a feeling of sublimity only when they are accompanied by assurance that some ideal goodness has shown its presence. And so we return to my claim that the sublime depends on idealization as well as imagination.[1]

In the modern world imagination and idealization have been misconstrued by many philosophers who sought to construct an ontology that hews closely to the findings of science. Ever since the so-called scientific revolution in the seventeenth century, empiricists as well as rationalists relegated phenomena such as imagination and idealization to a peripheral role in our knowledge, or even our perception, of the external world. We do not experience the objects of imagination or idealization, it was claimed, with the same directness as the sensory data that are normally given to inspection. Locke and other philosophers held that objective reality consists of primary qualities, like weight or size, and secondary qualities, like color or pitch, but not of pains, pleasures, or feelings in general. These were considered to be merely subjective responses to what was primary and secondary in our experience. It would seem to follow that effects of imagination and idealization must be only derivative reactions that lack the ultimacy of primary and secondary qualities.

Brentano, Husserl, and related phenomenologists contested this mode of analysis. They argued that meaning is given to consciousness with all the immediacy of sensation, and that sensation itself never occurs apart from the meaningfulness imparted by acts of evaluation and interpretation. Far from being derivative or completely subjective, meaning was already built into each moment of experience as it comes. This being the case, one can also say that imagination and idealization, as well as their continual interaction, are to be found in virtually all of human reality. They contribute to whatever coherence the world may have for us, and their operation helps to explain why it is, and how it is, that the world we experience does seem meaningful in some fashion and to some degree. Extending what the character in Shakespeare says about those who "are of imagination all compact," we can ascribe the same to everyone, and with respect to idealization as well in its joint creation of meaning.[2]

It is not enough, however, to claim that these three—imagination, idealization, meaningfulness—are direct and perennial contributors to the human world. Their contribution is highly variable from society to society, from individual to individual, and at different periods in a person's life. Though all, or most, of us may have a similar capacity for creating meaning through the agencies I have been describing, our particular creativity depends on delicate patterns of learning that must be acquired through education in its broadest sense. The family, the clan, the cultural milieu into which we are born instruct us in the rudiments of what is meaningful in the environment they represent, what is worthy of imaginative conception in accordance with a prescribed mode of idealization, and what directions our imagination should take in carrying out these normative demands.

This is not to say that we are *forced* to create meaning in conformity with the mandates of our society, but only that we are expected, and therefore naturally disposed, to do so. We are always free to rebel, to cast aside the web of presumptions into which we have been thrust by the arbitrary moment and localization of our birth. That invariably happens when a great man or woman appears upon the stage of life and declares, in variation of what Henry V says to Katharine in Shakespeare's play, "*I* am the maker of manners."[3] This efflorescence of freedom, which is available to some degree in all of us and at all times, together with the conventional constraints that define what we will even perceive as freedom, explains why it is that the world does not mean the same thing in different societies or uniformly within each society. Wittgenstein was right when he said that the world of the happy man is not the same as the world of one who is unhappy. How could it be? Their imaginations are performing in a contrary manner, expressing different values, different attitudes and interpretations, different *meanings* that they give to what might otherwise be identical in their experience.

Any actual examples of imagination and idealization, to say nothing of their interrelation, will therefore reveal the presence of both a prior, in some respects innate, potentiality and the greatly diversified development through time that a person enacts individually. Each lived experience will manifest not only differences accumulated as one's character evolves but also congenital tendencies resulting from chemical and physiological factors beyond control. When, in our outcast state, we bemoan the lack of many a virtue that some others have, we must always remind ourselves that they have doubtless inherited a brain and therefore a body that is capable of creating meaning in ways that are not available to us.

In his sonnet on this subject, Shakespeare ends by optimistically alluding to love as the remedy for one's sense of deficiency: "Haply I think on thee, and then my state, / Like to the lark at break of day arising, etc."[4] And it is true that love, which gives its own meaning to anything and everything, can lead to exquisitely vivid reawakening of both imagination and idealization. But our capacity for love is not unlimited, and it often falls short of what we might have hoped for. We end up as a composite of various elements: the generic potentiality in the human race, the specific portion of the realm of matter parceled out to each of us at birth, our individual immersion in one or another environment, our unique and personal development, and our luck or misfortune in encountering just the people or social circumstances whose trajectory in life happens to intersect with ours. The meaning that the world has for us, the overall quality that we have invested in it as the expression of our imagination and powers of idealization, is the precarious and thoroughly unpredictable outcome of these phenomena.

❉

In recent philosophy, with its great sensitivity to language as a distinctively human attribute, there is a tendency to assume that not the world but only linguistic structures can have meaning. This is a little like saying that not food but only breakfast, lunch, or dinner is nourishing. Language and its acquisition are supreme examples of how our species makes the world meaningful to itself, or rather how it makes a meaningful world *for* itself. But meaningfulness is not limited to linguistic aptitude. Language commands its own varieties of imagination and idealization without limiting their ability to fructify other aspects of human life.

Apart from category confusions about the nature of meaning, the linguistic thesis is worth criticizing because it deflects us from an adequate understanding of why art is so important in our existence. Language, like meaning as a whole, is natural in the sense of being an innate propensity definitive of this species. But art is more than that. Though it too is based on instinctual elements, some of them very deep in our being, and though it draws its materials directly from nature, art is a contrivance for going beyond nature. It adds to any resource we may have, including our linguistic capacity. As the word implies, art is artificial. It creates not only its own kind of meaning for what bombards our sensorium but also a supplemental world we can then experience on our own, often repeatedly.

The creativity in art is therefore very special. It liberates imagination from its mundane duties of making possible ordinary but often uninspired living. It does this by giving imagination free rein to wander at will beyond the limits ordained by practical necessity. In the context of art, imagination is permitted to create meaning in any way it can, in any interaction with idealization that it finds suitable for its purposes, and for the sake of virtually any effect that is inherently enjoyable to its audience. Such freedom is not to be found elsewhere in life. By offering this abstract opportunity and then enabling it to fulfill itself concretely, art achieves spiritual import, as I argue in the following chapters of this book.

While giving humankind access to this extraordinary type of liberation, art does more than just create meaning and enjoyment. It creates each of them in relation to the other. What is meaningful becomes enjoyable *through* art, enjoyment arising from our voluntary adherence to rules and artificial coordinates imposed by each particular art form as the basis of its unique creation of meaning. Art thereby yields consummation that results from relieving tensions within itself, as well as those that belong to the rest of life and could possibly be satisfied without its help. Through art the latter attain a refinement they would not have without it, while the former acquire a touch of nature that makes the artificial into the profoundly human.

In science or philosophy or the wisdom acquired through suffering, imagination plays as important a role as it does in art. These are all ways of creating meaning or finding it already created by others. But only in art is this process merged and integrated with consummatory possibilities that serve as an essential part of the experience. The scientist or philosopher may enjoy his work, especially when it fulfills his technical interests, as much as the artist enjoys his own. Yet only the artist creates with the explicit intention of making something that will be *enjoyable*, in one fashion or another. He is an expert in getting the real to appear ideal, not by falsifying its repulsive aspects but by presenting them within an aesthetic fabric that is consummatory in itself and possibly ideal. We may find the contents of a great tragedy painful, but the pain registers on our sensibility as enjoyable because it succeeds aesthetically, as relative to a work of art that has been carefully and beautifully constructed to give us a meaningful experience.

All authentic art makes this kind of transformation, and anything in life that approximates it becomes, to that degree, an artistic phenomenon, either a work of art or a product of artfulness. When we discuss spirituality in morals, I will suggest that all of life may duplicate this aesthetic achievement—assuming that we are sufficiently courageous and adequately endowed with the ability to pursue the noble art of living well. Thus far, not many of us have been able to do so.

HARMONIZATION
THROUGH ART

🌿

In distinguishing between meaning and happiness as I have, there is always a danger of overemphasizing the differences between them. Both belong to our life in nature, and each plays its part in the life of spirit that fulfills our natural potentialities. The preceding chapters of this book have explored the possibility that happiness and meaning may cooperate effectively, as in the workings of imagination and idealization. In being human faculties that institute cooperation of that sort, they enable art to serve as an exemplar of the spiritual life. By uniting our disparate cravings for meaning and for happiness, art transcends nature in the only way that nature can be transcended— by a harmonious completion within the natural, by consummation of natural impulses even though that lies beyond anything that nature can achieve independently.

These ideas about art as the harmonization of meaning with happiness, and as a culmination of the artificial which creates a fulfillment of what is native to our being and therefore nonartificial, require further clarification. We need to see more precisely how the interaction between imagination and idealization leads to consummatory goodness. This can happen only if there is a suitable accommodation between an organism and its environment. The aesthetic life, which pervades even utilitarian pursuits, is the human attempt to attain this kind of accommodation. But how do the coordinates we have been studying—meaning, happiness, imagination, idealization—structure and sustain it?

The difficulty of this question is compounded by the fact that art is not only artificial but *utterly* so. Possibly that is what Kant meant when he said that art is purposiveness without a purpose. When we experience art, however, either as creators or appreciators, it seems wholly natural and possibly closer to nature than most other human endeavors. Still, what could be more unnatural than the organization of sounds arranged in accordance with an abstract design and emitted by a chosen combination of manufactured instruments? Or paintings that present two-dimensional faces of men and women portrayed as if they were alive but obviously are not? Or a cinematic image that conveys a sense of motion while always being static? An artistic representation may look or sound natural, but it does not pulsate with the vibrant reality that even our least aesthetic experience comprises at every moment. If works of art put us "in touch" with nature, as they often do, it is because they digest and reconstitute it through the imagination for the sake of consummations we could not have in any other experience. This means, however, that *through*, not despite, the artificiality of art we live in nature and in accordance with it. How is that possible?

To begin with, we must recognize that every organism is programmed to want what will satisfy. All animate being manifests a search for self-realization, not as sophisticated and elaborate as it is for us but similar in some respects. Human beings are unique (as far as we can tell) in having learned how to generate progressively new and largely artificial means of attaining consummatory values. Among these, the enjoyment of art contributes to a happiness that may be the most reliable and enduring type available to us. But also, artistic consummations are meaningful throughout their artificiality.

These basic ideas will be my guide in this and the following chapter. On the face of it, the suggestion that art may provide a greater and more pervasive happiness than anything else in life might easily seem outrageous. Even when defended by a master such as Proust, the doctrine sounds like a form of special pleading on the part of those who have failed to achieve any other happiness. Its plausibility results from the fact that the aesthetic can give value-laden meaning to every part of life or nature that it chooses to include within itself. That is a major accomplishment in the universe. It is worth noting if only because we usually take it for granted, like a second nature to which we were born.

Art creates a unique, and especially beguiling, happiness by fabricating a self-enclosed realm of meaningful awareness, a little world that has been made with explicit enjoyment as its goal. In first nature we seek for consummation but can never know in advance whether our search is realistic under the circumstances. Art systematically provides conditions in which the pursuit always makes sense. That is a service art accords to all humanity: it offers both meaning and consummation to anyone who has learned to appreciate its artificial constructs. Nothing else in life does that, and everything that does do it is ipso facto an artistic achievement.

This way of characterizing art is not self-evident. In a representational medium, for instance, one may think that the function and the virtue of aesthetic creativity consists in proferring for renewed delectation something we have already seen or heard. On this view, the meanings of Monet's haystacks were already in the world and had only to be portrayed with accuracy and with skill: the painter succeeded because he had the requisite talent for depicting prior meaning.

To say this, however, is to ignore the many ways in which art introduces meanings that are entirely its own. The haystacks that a local farmer may have seen in the same location are ontologically different from the ones that Monet presents. For the farmer, and for Monet himself in his unpainterly moments, the haystacks meant something that results from agricultural labor, a favorable climate, a desire to provide fodder for the livestock, and so on. Monet the artist does not turn his back on these meanings. For him, as for the farmer, they are needed to understand the realities embodied in the haystacks he is painting. But as a painter Monet intuits that meanings of this sort are only values the world has furnished his imagination for it to use exactly as it wishes. His creativity consists in the ability to make these given values meaningful in a further dimension defined by the techniques of his art and the parameters of his personal vision.

The haystacks that we see on the canvas may or may not look like haystacks that the farmer saw. As participants in a work of art, however, they acquire the integral meaning bestowed upon them by the painter. Assuming that he is gifted as an artist, we may expect this meaning to yield its own type of goodness. It satisfies a sensory or emotional or cognitive need relevant to itself and fully realized within its medium. To that extent, all media, and indeed all activities, that combine consummation and meaning are equally artistic. In taking note of this, our language is often metaphoric. But the metaphor is based on our recognition that art amplifies our search for happiness by giving its own importance to whatever it presents, and that this occurs through imaginative meanings that art creates and then exploits for ends that are explicitly enjoyable.

✳

At this point one might object that much of art does not make us happy. Does anyone relish the massacres and ghastly executions in works by Goya or Picasso, or the tormented visages in Munch or Kollwitz? Though bucolic scenes or melodious tunes provide happiness for a while, how could one pretend that the unpleasant sights and sounds in art do anything of the sort?

Those who raise this kind of objection are right to insist that art is frequently designed to shock and even offend us. Art is a part of life; it is not a separate reality subsisting through illusion and magical wish fulfillment. On the contrary, art draws its inspiration from what it encounters in the ordinary world to which we all belong. In making that world meaningful through its own imaginative devices, it cannot deviate completely from observable facts. And one of the facts that all reflective people recognize is the vast amount of suffering that pervades our reality.

Art is free to interpret the calamities of life however it desires. Its divergent interpretations issue into the varied meanings that different works can realize with total legitimacy. While appreciating the authenticity of realistic details, disquieting as they may be, the spectator also delights in the transformations that art effects by imposing its own meaning upon them. Within the aesthetic object, these meanings attain a completeness that we experience as a consummation and a source of happiness. We are not rendered happy by seeing or hearing the sorrows that animate creatures endure, but we may and do enjoy the artist's portrayal of them.

Mozart understood this very well. Describing, in a letter to his father, an aria he has just written for Osmin in *The Abduction from the Seraglio*, Mozart prides himself on having captured the anger, the fury, the harsh and uncontrollable malice of this thwarted petty tyrant. We have all known men who behave like Osmin. As members of society, they are realities that do not further anyone's happiness. But the Osmin we observe in Mozart's opera is a buffoon whose vicious deportment elicits laughter rather than fear or disgust. Though his raging is a serious danger to those subjected to it in the story, it has been given a different kind of meaning by his comedic role. We in the audience enjoy his violent manner and are never really frightened by it. Moreover, his feelings are expressed through sounds—some of which he utters and some emitted by the orchestra—that conform to harmonic laws the human ear finds pleasurable in themselves.

In his letter Mozart delights in the fact that he has remained faithful to psychological truth while also encasing it within the aesthetic goodness of beautiful music:

> As Osmin's rage gradually increases, there comes (just when the aria seems to be at an end) the allegro assai, which is in a totally different measure and in a different key; this is bound to be very effective. For just as a man in such a towering rage oversteps all the bounds of order, moderation, and propriety and completely forgets himself, so must the music too forget itself. But as passions, whether violent or not, must never be expressed in such a way as to excite disgust, and as music, even in the most terrible situations, must never offend the ear, but must please the hearer, or, in other words, must never cease to be *music*,

I have gone from F (the key in which the aria is written), not into a remote key, but into a related one, not, however into its nearest relative D minor, but into the more remote A minor.[1]

Elsewhere I have discussed this aria as an example of musical metaphor in opera.[2] Here I want to emphasize Mozart's belief that music must "please the hearer" even in the presentation of unpleasant emotionality. We can agree about that, but we may also want to add that musical pleasure differs greatly from hearer to hearer and from one composition to another. Arts such as opera exist because human beings have learned how to make patterns of sound and sight that please us in works that would lead to everlasting happiness if only they could be savored continuously throughout our lives. Art as a concept, and as an institution, expresses our hope to create through its diverse media a renewable happiness that exists only as a result of artistic creativity.

Pleasure, for instance auditory pleasure, can occur in nature without the intervention of any arts. Being fortunate enough to live in the neighborhood of a phoebe bird, we might relish and regularly enjoy its two-note song. Such simple pleasures come upon us gratuitously in nature and may conduce to happiness. But the bird is not an artist. However much we like listening to its cheerful legato, it is not performing a musical composition invented for our enjoyment. That takes an aesthetic imagination phoebes do not have. In his Sixth Symphony, Beethoven employs sounds that resemble but do not replicate those of nightingale, quail, and cuckoo. In itself, a replication would not be art, which always strives to create *new* sources of consummatory pleasure. Hence Beethoven uses instruments that are not only artificial but also parts of an orchestral ensemble that offers musical innovations quite distinct from anything one hears in field or woodland.

The joy that people get from creating, performing, or just experiencing works of art does not need to be documented. It results from the gratification of sensory, emotional, and cognitive capabilities that have been carried to fulfillment within a setting created for their harmonious integration. But while this orientation toward consummation is a necessary condition for art to exist, it is not sufficient. Art is more than entertainment alone. It is also meaningful in ways that are sometimes of the greatest importance.

There is a sense in which Archibald MacLeish was right when he stated that "A poem should not mean/but be."³ We must remember, however, that MacLeish said this within a poem, which is itself a contrivance for making supremely meaningful statements such as that one. If the remark had occurred by itself and as a factual proposition, it would strike us as either trivial or absurd. It is trivial to tell us that poetry differs from prose since poetry often goes beyond the communication of literal meanings. It is absurd to suggest that the words in poetry do not mean anything at all.

The pregnant import of MacLeish's aphorism is related to its being the last lines in his poem. It is therefore itself meaningful as a frame or provocative closure that reorients our attentive experience, turning it back into the lines that preceded it. We are thereby encouraged to revel in the aesthetic texture of the artwork to which the last lines belong. The *be*ing of this texture is worthy of our admiration, MacLeish believes, and we may too. But we would not care about the specific entity that is the poem he has written unless we felt that something highly meaningful had been created in the process of giving us the rare and wonderful enjoyment afforded by such uses of language.

There are two kinds of meaning that are present in art and harmonized with the happiness art constantly seeks to foster. One kind of meaning is inherent, the other referential. The inherent meaning issues from the formal and material elements that are structural to every art. In addition to aesthetic principles the arts may all have in common, each of them unites form and matter in different ways that define our relevant experience of them. To understand the inherent meaning of music one must study key patterns, the relationship between chords or tonal clusters, the variations of pitch and timbre. An understanding of what is inherently meaningful in painting requires sensitivity to visual design, and to the relative brightness, hue, and saturation of colors juxtaposed as if they were trying to communicate with one another.

Through its referential meaning, art moves beyond the internal configurations that make it inherently meaningful. Referential meaning is art using its inherent meanings for the sake of portraying or commenting upon the outside world, projecting feelings about it and delving into human realities that may be unapproachable otherwise. Articulating its optional perspectives, in accordance with the form and matter of each particular medium, art often arouses in its audience emotional and cathartic reactions to our condition as animate beings. It sometimes penetrates to an overall vision that affects people as profoundly philosophical without being analytically technical or discursive. Even art that may be called sad or tragic can thereby contribute to happiness.

Since I am not writing a treatise on aesthetics, I will bypass many of the important questions about the nature of material, formal, and representational elements in art. It will be useful, however, to see how referential and inherent meanings are related to each other. Returning to the example of Osmin's aria, we may wonder how the pleasure of listening to such music can be simultaneously meaningful in both modalities. Of course, just knowing that Osmin is raging and somewhat out of control can add to our enjoyment of what is happening in the music. We perceive that its rhythmic pattern mimics his vehement, stamping movements, and we can see why the modulations in key that Mozart mentions might have seemed uncontrolled at the time he was writing. This is all good fun and quite amusing, but how does it tell us about the world or express our feelings toward it? What kind of referential meaning results from the inherent values in the music?

It would be a mistake to think that the referential meaning in Osmin's aria is either the same as or completely different from meanings that appear in the rest of life. A psychologist might explain Osmin's fury in terms of aggressiveness and male competition for the possession of desirable females. This kind of analysis is not irrelevant to an understanding of the aria. In fact, we could hardly savor the fullness of its meaning without some such consideration.

At the same time, Mozart and his librettist presuppose that we know what a jealous man is like. They are not writing a textbook. We enter the theater with a template of ideas that the artists can draw upon and modify as they wish. In doing so, they *increase* our sophistication, and even in this comic opera about life in a Turkish harem we are left with an edifying contrast between Osmin's kind of behavior and the more humane conduct that the pasha exemplifies at the end. But in itself this quasi-philosophical statement about the moral vicissitudes of human nature does not reveal what is unique about the referential meaning of Mozart's music.

Whatever his capacities for abstract thought, the artist must attend at every moment to the inherent meanings in the aesthetic presentation. That is why Mozart in his letter emphasizes the inventiveness of using different keys but lays no claim to originality in the ideas about Osmin's emotions. In great works of art there is often much psychological and philosophical profundity, but it always issues *out of* the inherent meanings. On the other hand, the inherent meanings are not the only ones that matter aesthetically. To relish Mozart's talent as a parodist, we must recognize his cleverness in using formal and material devices to say something about the world. To that extent, our aesthetic experience includes an appreciation of the referential meanings that Mozart creates through his sonic art. He cannot tell us much about jealous men in the manner of an empirical investigator, and yet he conveys an understanding of such persons that few scientists can ever approximate. But how is that possible?

Apart from the psychological insights it provides, Mozart's musical caricature allows us to probe the qualitative nature of what it is like to be a jealous male. Not only does the music "please the hearer" and provide inherent meanings that are a source of enjoyment, but also their enjoyability adapts the frightening potentiality of Osmin's outburst to a staged performance that is both consummatory and a revelation of human feeling. It is not just a question of making Osmin seem and sound pleasantly buffoonish. If the work of art were a tragedy, like Verdi's *Otello* or Shakespeare's *Othello*, the referential meanings would be different from Mozart's while depending upon inherent meanings in a comparable fashion. We do not laugh at the screaming and the weeping of Otello because we do not interpret Verdi's music as parodistic. It nevertheless succeeds in accommodating within its own harmonic discipline sounds that jealous men not infrequently make in the real world as a means of venting what they are undergoing emotionally.

Because the referential meanings in Mozart and Verdi (or Shakespeare in his different art form) emanate from their own inherent meanings, we are able to experience much that would not be available to us through science or other types of knowledge. We may not acquire much information from the music, but we will be able to *feel* what jealous men are like. By writing music that is outlandish, and therefore humorous, Mozart enables us to enjoy and observe, at a safe distance, the ludicrous state that jealousy can put a person in. By offering music of another sort, Verdi causes us to sense and to share, if we are empathetic, the agony that also belongs to this condition. Being ludicrous and being agonized are realities that we may possibly understand best—at least, in their qualitative aspects—by seeing and hearing them expressed in works of art.

In his attempt to show how the aesthetic transcends nature, Sartre says that the art object is "unreal." This is a tantalizing idea, since no one can doubt that works of art are not *in* reality until such time as an artist has arranged to put them there. Relying on the imagination as it does, art often entrances us with aesthetic effects that are *imaginary*. I employ that word in its ordinary connotation, though sharpened for the sake of the distinction I wish to draw. The imaginary is a fictional, and to that extent unrealistic, use of imagination. But even in works of art explicitly devoted to make-believe, the imaginary generally serves as a backdrop or invented setting for something the imagination has taken from a prior reality. Being artificial and innovative by nature, art readily avails itself of anything we may wish to imagine through the imaginary. But in order to register on us, as creatures whose sheer survival necessitates our perceiving, and sometimes appropriating, whatever occurs in the surrounding factuality of nature, the imaginary must always presuppose a world that is indeed real and not merely imagined. Unless it showed awareness of nature, art could not carry out its mission of going *beyond* nature.

The demonstration of this mission is itself an important element in aesthetic experience. The human mind, operating here through the imagination and its deployment in art, seems to feel a need to test itself against reality, to assert its indefeasible autonomy despite its dependence on nature, to show that while it knows what actually exists it remains forever free to alter that reality in its own fashion.

Since powers of the mind are highly circumscribed, there will always be a limited number of things that it can do to change the content or the course of nature. But though imagination is also finite (we cannot imagine what a round square would be like), it has enormous scope within the dimensions that are available to it. The imaginary even allows it to entertain ideas of what we know to be impossible—potions that turn princes into frogs or cause girls in wonderland to become very tall or very small, as the case may be. Insofar as it relies not only on the imagination but specifically on the imaginary, art includes the unreal as well as the real.

Still, there are important questions to be asked. For one thing, why does the mind choose this cumbersome method of asserting its dignity, pretending that it is independent of nature although it has no being without it? Would it not be simpler to enjoy nature directly rather than going to all the trouble of inventing imaginary possibilities that take us beyond it? Enjoyment is itself an appropriation that enriches our condition as just the creatures that we are. Spinoza believed that pleasure always manifests our natural ability to sustain ourselves. If we feel exhilarated by vivid sunsets, we need only watch them on a clear enough evening. Why paint or photograph them, why take any interest in what an artist has painted or photographed as an expression of his or her experience, since we can have a similar one, without the artist's intervention and at no expense? Do we not capture the scene just by seeing and enjoying its occurrence ourselves? Instead of living the substitute life of art, why not just *live*? Life being short, why not concentrate on enjoyments that do not require the tedious training and preparation that art usually demands?

Moreover, the very nature of art is notoriously deficient. Life is fluid in its passage through time, three-dimensional in its spatiality, and dynamic in ways that art cannot attain. And though it may want to do so, we may well wonder whether art can ever "capture" reality. Many aestheticians have said it can, but much of what they allege is problematic. The arts of film and photography are the most likely candidates as capturers of reality, since they can copy and even reproduce components in it that normally escape unaided human vision. In his theory of "total cinema" André Bazin suggests that, more than any other art, film aspires to a complete duplication of reality. But that is only a metaphoric way of saying that film imitates reality in some relevant details, which is not at all the same as duplicating it. And anyhow, why should we make an ersatz replica of an original that is always with us, accessible and even inescapable by the fact of our mere existence?

From this perspective, it is not surprising that artists have sometimes been treated like people who pander to a human frailty, the addictive need to inhabit an unreal and sometimes illusory world of aesthetic possibles rather than living fruitfully in nature itself. That artists should behave as they do is understandable: they are paid for their services, just as prostitutes and drug dealers are. They are usually hooked themselves on this common preference for virtual but inauthentic reality. Can their particular kind of life be recommended for others, or even justified in itself?

As a traitor to his own artistic genius, Plato argued that art should be banned from the ideal state because it is only an image of an image and thus greatly removed from ultimate reality. Can one not, in a similar vein, suggest that men and women fortify their minds not by imagining what is nonexistent but instead by cultivating aptitudes that help them to enjoy the beauties that do exist, at every moment, in the world of actuality?

If one did say this, one would be misconstruing the function of the imaginary and therefore of art itself. Although they can be misused, like every other source of goodness, these do not deprive us of our capacity to enjoy reality. On the contrary, they arouse and also cultivate perceptual and cognitive powers of the mind needed for any consummatory appreciation of nature. Art does that in the pursuit of its own artificial goals, but they cannot be wholly separated from our search for natural beauties. Though we could not fully enjoy a Turner sunset unless we had seen others in nature, once we learn how to look at Turner's imaginary display of light and color we see something in nature's prototype that exists for us only because of the painting we have experienced aesthetically.

All art functions in a comparable manner. We might even say that it is nature re-creating itself, not as a denial of whatever beauty or goodness has already emerged but as an augmentation of it. From the purely human point of view, art is serendipitous: at one and the same time, it allows us to find and create new consummations while escaping the price that nature often exacts for those, in love or sexuality, for instance, that it also yields but sometimes withholds. We can have this serendipity only through the imaginary element of imagination, which is to say, through art in all its many creative varieties.

I spoke earlier about ideas of the impossible being "entertained" by the imaginary. How is this to be explained? We never have an actual image of a round square. It cannot be seen in the mind's eye in the way that an image of my departed cat Catullus is recurrently present to me. Still, I am able to use the term *round square* quite easily. It rolls off my tongue and through my consciousness. But even though it refers to something imaginary, I cannot comprehend it as I do with other language that connotes imaginary entities. I know what it is like for there to be a unicorn, and I am not surprised when people say that these fictional entities may have once existed. Round square is different. I do not comprehend what it is for something to be round and square in the same sense and at the same time. I only know what *round* and *square* mean, and that physical properties like them (though not them in particular) are combinable with one another. What nevertheless remains is a *feeling* about roundness and squareness and the attempt to unite them in the imagination. That there are such feelings reveals a great deal about the imaginary as well as about imagination and the ontology of art.

Approaching art as imaginary, and then the imaginary as an expression of feelings related to the imagination, can help us to avoid mistakes that aestheticians have often made. Most dramatically perhaps, it shows the futility of identifying imagination with our ability to have or evoke images. Turning away from a gorgeous sunset, we may see an afterimage of the orange glob dipping into the horizon; watching a movie, we perceive a photographic image that may closely resemble something we have encountered in our own experience; listening to Debussy's *La Mer*, we may have an auditory image of crashing waves such as those we have heard at some time in the past; and so on. These are all effects gathered within the portmanteau concept of what we call imagination, and they play a part in both the creation and appreciation of art. But philosophers who have thought that imagination is primarily an image-making faculty were misled by something like a picture, as Wittgenstein would say. The image making through which imagination does occasionally operate tells us little about the imaginative qualities of art, and even less about the role of the imaginary. To understand the nature and the importance of art, we need to explore characteristics of the imaginary that have nothing to do with the making or recalling of images.

The key to these characteristics is the fact that the imaginary expresses feelings without giving a literal representation of them. Consider psychologists or psychiatrists who study scientifically feelings that someone might undergo at various moments. To do their work as professionals, they rely on imagination as well as careful observation and rigorous analysis. They may even introduce imaginary case studies that enable them to give a more clearly delineated account than if they followed a purely empirical methodology. But for their purposes the imaginary must always remain secondary and incidental. They are trying to reach not artistic truths but rather factual conclusions that are independent of the imaginary. They wish to present or process data as these exist in the world, apart from themselves and their own feelings about them. It is irrelevant that the subject of their investigation is an emotion or cluster of feelings. It could have been anything else as far as their scientific intentions are concerned.

For the artist and his or her audience the situation is significantly different. Though they have no need to *falsify* reality, they are not primarily interested in literal representations of it. Being attuned to imaginary possibilities, art is exempt from any such necessity. It has its own way of dealing with reality. Instead of limiting itself to what is factual, it expresses feelings that communicate indirectly what it considers important in the world. That is why the imaginary, which may summon actual impossibilities that nevertheless feel to us as if they could be the real thing, constitutes the type of imagination that art generally chooses.

I can illustrate this with an example that Sartre has used. He analyzes the impersonation of Maurice Chevalier by the actress Franconay. Though Chevalier was tall and slender, Sartre remarks, we are not deterred by Franconay's being short, plump, and of a different gender. Her impersonation works because she is able to superimpose what Sartre calls the "Chevalier-feeling" upon the "Chevalier-appearance." The latter is required in order to identify her subject, but it uses just a few conventional signs—Chevalier's straw hat, his stick, his flashing smile. These signs are only secondary in the artistry of Franconay's impersonation. That depends on her ability to convey the Chevalier-feeling, which Sartre describes as Chevalier's manner, his style, the meaning of what he says or does, and in general his uniquely personal self-presentation.[4]

Sartre leaves the analysis there, but we should try to take it further. Whose feeling is the "Chevalier-feeling"? Presumably not Chevalier's, since he may present himself one way and yet feel something very different, even while he makes his presentation. As a performing artist, he conveyed that blend of romantic ardor and sensuous insouciance that gave his singing its particular kind of charm. But how was any of this related to what he actually felt? Was he himself both ardent and insouciant? Appearing that way in public, was he being sincere or just playacting, as people often do whether or not they are on stage? Was he possibly as cynical as Don Juan in all his protestations of love? And, in principle, who can give a reliable answer to questions such as these? Could Chevalier or his devoted mother or any of the women he made love to? But at best even they could only tell us about Chevalier's feelings, not about the nature of the Chevalier-feeling. As long as the clarification of that continues to elude us, Sartre's account is not very helpful.

In an attempt to avoid this impasse, I suggest that the feelings that explain the imaginary and its function in art are feelings in the audience that an accomplished artist can manipulate to good effect. Franconay knew how people reacted to the Chevalier they saw on stage. She had seen his performances herself, and to that extent she too was a member of what she imagined her audience to be. Drawing upon her own responses, she could intuit what the others must have felt while watching Chevalier perform. To impersonate him, she had to superimpose these collective feelings upon the Chevalier-appearance. In the process she did more than just express the feelings that she and others had *about* his appearance. That might have been legitimate in itself, but it would have diminished the imaginary and vitiated her art. Instead she incorporated in her own appearance whatever it was in Chevalier's that conveyed the style and meaning considered uniquely his. She thereby created in the audience feelings that were fictional, feelings ostensibly directed toward Chevalier but actually directed toward her pretending at that moment to be Chevalier.

Though spectators have only a feeling for what a performing artist's style and meaning are, that was sufficient for Franconay's employment of the imaginary. Her art as a mimic consisted in her ability to get the audience to have a make-believe experience, treating her selective words and actions as they would have Chevalier's.

✳

Because art defines itself in terms of the imaginary aspect of imagination, and because the imaginary tolerates impossibilities and articulates feelings based on inexhaustive evidence, art must always have an approach to truth quite different from what one finds in science or philosophy. I develop that suggestion in the next chapter. I introduce the idea here as a step toward understanding the relationship between art and nature.

Assuming I am right in saying that art cannot capture reality by re-presenting it, even when it succeeds in giving a telling representation of it, we must determine how reality can be captured. I think of Picasso's aggressive personality, his bulging eyes engaged in a confrontational struggle with the world he wished to dominate. He used his brush or pencil as an extension of his thrusting and invasive attitude, much as a swordsman uses his weapon to conquer or subdue whatever has aroused his militant fervor. A realistic portrayal would not have sufficed for the mastery and possession that Picasso sought. He wanted to break the visual scene into pieces, as great poets do with preformed verbiage they inherit, and then, like them, to recombine the fragments in a work that conveyed his feelings about the original reality. That excursion into the imaginary, indeed the impossible—unreal women with both eyes on one side of their nose—was an assertion of his imperious desire to force nature to his will.

In Picasso's case the effort succeeded, to the glory of art. It did so not only because it expressed feelings that many people in the twentieth century have had toward nature but also because there is much about unabating reality that is best shown through an artificial and imaginative repudiation of it. Spirit often exists in defiance of the nature from which it arises. It proudly proclaims that even if we can do little more than scream, as in the painting by Munch, we refuse to acquiesce in the misery that nature is capable of inflicting on us all.

At the same time, spirit can revel in the consummations that nature allows for those who divine its inner secrets. Even the most angry and rebellious artist, if he is worthy of his medium, will delight in the sight, the sound, the feel, and possibly the smell of the materials he has chosen for his artwork. These are usually given the artist by nature itself, like a mother who mingles seductive kindliness with her restraining edicts. The artist's creativity appears in selecting which materials to use, and to what end.

By accepting these implements, the artist is acquiescing in nature's gifts, even if he finally throws them at the canvas as a means of asserting his autonomy. That assertion, whether or not it is rebellious, can give him access to the life of spirit. In making his gesture, he enables the imaginary to concoct possibilities of the imagination that not only transcend actuality but also enunciate truths about it that may be unknowable apart from art. Archimedes said that with a long enough lever he could move the earth. With the imaginary as their lever, artists can and do dislodge the nature without which neither they nor anything else could exist. Archimedes' achievement, if he could manage it, would have been a stupendous feat in the realm of matter. What art effects, in my analogy, is an equally significant event in spirit as well as nature. Although we take it as a commonplace of daily life, its mere occurrence is a wonderment. That is what I wish to consider further in the next chapter.

ART & SPIRITUALITY

In this chapter I wish to explore two phenomena that enable art to enrich the life of spirit: the relationship between art and consummation, and the unique type of truthfulness about reality that art provides when it is most successful. Once these are better understood, we may infer that while art is not the only type of spirituality it can nevertheless serve as a model or explanatory principle for all other types.

✻

In considering the relationship between art and consummation, we may benefit from the philosophy of John Dewey. In *Art as Experience* Dewey describes the aesthetic as a "quality" that life acquires when it attains an appropriate completion within itself. This quality occurs through the having of what Dewey calls *"an* experience," which he explains by saying that "we have *an* experience when the material experienced runs its course to fulfillment."[1] Dewey's subsequent depiction of this benign possibility indicates that the defining quality is a sense of unity, integration, and ongoing process inhering in life at its healthiest. The aesthetic, and therefore the work of art that results from it as well as making it available to others, is thus portrayed as a consummation coherent with any forms or materials that lead to organic self-fulfillment. In the last chapter of his book, Dewey sums up this basic idea as follows: "Art is a quality that permeates an experience; it is not, save by a figure of speech, the experience itself. Esthetic experience is always more than esthetic. In it a body of matters and meanings, not in themselves esthetic, *become* esthetic as they enter into an ordered rhythmic movement toward consummation."[2]

Dewey's statement is problematic in more than one respect. Characterizing the aesthetic as he does, Dewey would seem to mean by "quality" a property within some experience. Listening to a birdsong, we feel a quality of joy or well-being that permeates the auditory occasion. This is not a quality in the song itself. But Dewey would also seem to be talking about the art object, as if it were comparable to an experience and could have qualities of the same sort. When he analyzes the way in which materials, form, and representational content are unified in a work of art, Dewey appears to be referring to something more than just our experience of them. He suggests that these elements cannot be aesthetic unless they reach their own completion in themselves and as components in a work of art.

This difficulty becomes particularly troublesome when we wonder what is meant by the consummation that is central to Dewey's view. If I am right in thinking that art harmonizes the creation of meaning with the search for happiness and therefore enjoyment, it is important to know wherein lies its consummatory quality. In experience as a whole, enjoyability usually derives from some fulfillment of an organic need or impulse. Getting what we want, we attain a gratification that quiets our restlessness for a while. A life that consisted of nothing but consummations of this type would be a perfectly happy one. A work of art that added greatly to our quest for meaning, while also providing consummatory goods within its own formal and material structure, would approximate an ideal of what we may call perfect art. This might also be what Dewey has in mind. If so, the title of his book could be interpreted to mean *Art As [the Basis of Truly Consummatory] Experience*.

Reading Dewey in this fashion, we preserve the radical empiricism that is latent in all his thought but avoid his dubious remarks about an artistic *quality*. Any object, and any attributes pertaining to it, would be artistic insofar as they yield whatever consummations people care about. Having established this, however, we would still need to determine what a consummation is and how it attains its possible spirituality.

In modern parlance, the word *consummation* often connotes a sexual, possibly orgasmic, completion. Somewhat legalistically perhaps, a marriage is said to remain unconsummated until sexual intercourse occurs between the spouses. This example is useful for our purpose because one might have thought that the consummation of marriage involves more than just bodily penetration. Does it not require a lasting bond of love or fidelity, for instance? But these are more amorphous, and harder to understand, than the mere enactment of sex acts related to procreation and the possible making of a family. The deed itself, what Shakespeare's character calls the deed of darkness, is only an event in material nature and scarcely spiritual in itself. For love or marriage to be consummated there would have to be a network of operative human meanings that transcend the purely physical. That kind of consummation provides a foundation for life that is meaningful to us as human beings who are striving for happiness distinctive of our species.

We all recognize this when we watch "lower" organisms, as we call them, engage in coitus. They seem to accept their respective roles within the ordained mode of reproduction as routine factualities of no emotional or personal importance. Even in their courtship and ritualized behavior, they *submit* to sex rather than cultivating it as an opportunity for individual fulfillment. Having made the programmed contact, they go about the business of life as if nothing special has occurred, at least not to them. Though we can say that their sexual urges have been consummated, that sounds oddly metaphoric. In any event, it is a different type of consummation from the one that we human beings generally seek when we engage in sexuality. We often detach the consummatory experience of sex from reproductive possibilities, and we characteristically imbue it with societal standards, such as those of interpersonal love or marital oneness.

All the same, we know that the "art of sex" thrives on special-ized techniques and pertains to ideals of performance that are not delimited by love, marriage, or what usually counts as social value. The sexuality of human beings can be crude, casual, and largely meaningless. It can be for us more brutal than among the creatures we foolishly consider brutes. But the art of sex precludes all that. It entails an imaginative concern about refinement in taste, pleasur-ability, and collateral excitation that changes a mechanical proce-dure into an experience of delight and mutual enjoyment. It is this transformation of the natural into the beautiful which reveals the spirituality of art, whether it be the art of sex or love or any of the traditional arts referred to as either "fine" or "useful." Consumma-tion is the unifying theme, but it is consummation interwoven with our human capacity for imagination and idealization.

In previous chapters I emphasized the role that imagination and idealization play in the creation of meaning. Without them, both individually and in their relation to each other, nothing in life would be meaningful for us. Without them we could not lead purposive lives; and without purposiveness and the ability to get beyond it through a gratuitous bestowal of value, we would not experience the world as having the meaning it ordinarily has for us. But also imagination and idealization are fundamental in our striving to experience happiness that consists of consummations that satisfy *because* they are profoundly human. Even in the matter of sexual activity, the person who can turn it into an art form is usually one whose imagination is rich enough to intuit extensive modes of enjoyment coherent with valued and idealized responses that are awakened in one's partner as well as in oneself. Among the different arts there will be vastly different uses to which imagination and idealization may be put, but their constant and operative pres-ence is needed throughout.

One reason that aesthetics has made relatively little progress as a philosophical discipline is the difficulty one always encounters in trying to determine which are the relevant consummations in arts such as music, literature, dance, or painting. Nature has prepared us for the art of sex by giving us organic drives, which often function in obeyance to hormonal commands. Artfulness then consists in carrying out this prescribed behavior with a maximum of elegance, kindliness, and hedonic sophistication. But the fine arts have structures of another sort. They are more artificial, and considerably more abstract, than the art of sex—or, for that matter, the art of cooking a good meal or serving it graciously. Although painting, sculpture, music, and the like could not exist without physical materials—sounds and colors that are pleasing to our sense organs— these arts are free to use their materials more or less as they wish. That being the case, how can we know which are the appropriate consummations in each medium? Aestheticians may debate about rules that should govern some particular art form, but there can be no doubting the fact that, unlike arts related to sex or cooking or even rug weaving, the fine arts are at liberty to reject virtually any rule ordained by nature or convention.

There are various ways in which the fine arts exercise their freedom, and therefore different modes of consummation that they can offer. First, they search out sensory materials that are available to the artist not only as the means by which he or she can achieve the ends of beauty but also as the conveyors of whatever effects will seem interesting. In abstract painting or nonprogrammatic music, for instance, the work of art often concentrates its energies on colors or sonic values that have never been seen or heard before. Even if they are not inherently beautiful, these new creations can arrest our attention and provide satisfactions that have unique and lasting impact. More than forty years ago I visited an exhibit in Paris of Gauguin paintings, including the one entitled *Nevermore*. I remember relatively few things from that period in my life, but the saffron color of the pillow in this painting has vividly remained in my consciousness ever since. I do not believe I had ever seen that hue before, and I doubt that I have seen it since. It affected some responsiveness in my physiology that was strongly attuned to it.

It activated a visual consummation I still cherish even though, at present, I am not sure I would now consider that shade of yellow either beautiful or especially interesting.

This example can be duplicated in each of the arts, for they all employ materials that are freely chosen for their hedonic or affective qualities as well as for their ability to fit into a formal structure and to serve a referential function. A vibrant color or ear-ravishing sound gives an immediate consummation of the same order as a delicious morsel or pleasant touch. In each case one must be well equipped physiologically while also being aesthetically alert. Regardless of what the sensory modality is, one must know how to look or listen or taste or feel, and one must be able to benefit from this susceptibility. The arts are all devices for maximizing such consummations, though they do so differently and with different criteria of importance.

Even in the most abstract works of art, nonfigurative sculpture for instance, materials and their relevant consummations appear in the context of consummations that are more than just material. In addition to the pleasure given by a color or texture, there is the pleasure of the form that it shows forth while imbuing that form with the vitality only matter has. Formal consummations may also be immediate and organic, but as an enrichment of our aesthetic experience their enjoyability is likely to derive from some inherent meaningfulness of their own.

As I described it earlier, inherent meaning in a work of art depends on the rules and inner unity that give that work its structure. The resulting consummations issue from our recognition of the artist's success in putting together this art object as he has. We delight in his expertise, in the skill or inventiveness with which he solves the many problems he encountered in creating his work of art. Our appreciation is itself a consummatory enrichment. Seeing how a talented person thinks, and therefore makes aesthetic decisions, fulfills at second hand our own desire to be an artist. At least, we learn how creativity operates, and that is a source of happiness as well as comprehension. It is the kind of joy we feel in observing any animate creature that is strong and successful within the potentialities of its own existence. This effect is most evident in our response to healthy, growing babies or pups of any sort.

Over and above the consummations related to inherent meaning, there are those engendered by what I called the referential meanings that works of art also have. They are of many kinds. First, and most obviously, art tells us about the world. Although the fine arts do not usually present themselves as a form of explicit instruction, their reliance on the imaginary aspect of imagination enables them to give valid information without being didactic. Realistic novels such as Zola's *Nana* or Joyce's *Ulysses* are both fictional and a purveyor of knowledge about the society, the locale, and many of the persons they portray. The pleasure of living vicariously in the depicted world—the Paris or Dublin that establishes the background of the narrative and sometimes becomes a major element in it—affords a consummatory experience comparable to what one gets from reading history or sociology. In *The Experimental Novel* Zola claimed that his fiction had the virtue of being journalistic, even scientific, in its ability to convey literal truths about people and events that actually existed and were not fanciful concoctions of a romanticizing imagination.

And yet, even realistic novels are make-believe, which should remind us of the other consummations that they can also provide. In these fictional works we enjoy the unreality of what is thoroughly imaginary, for that allows us to pick and choose all possibilities of nature that serve our creative purposes, either as artists or as members of an audience. The Paris and Dublin in the writings of Zola or Joyce are literary constructions despite their authentic and almost archeological basis in reality. They are rearrangements of a prior being, and in that respect similar to El Greco's Toledo. The reader's consummatory experience springs from the realization that much of nature can be understood only through a highly selective and *re*-creative approach to what is given in ordinary experience.

Although Zola's theory is confused at this point, his including the word *experimental* in the title of his book seems inspired. An experiment, whether or not scientific, is a paradigm of the mind imposing imaginative procedures upon the world in order to uncover secrets of nature that might otherwise be permanently hidden. When the effort succeeds, we glory in the power of our imagination as well as our intellect; and this consummatory outcome is substantially the same in art as it is in science.

❋

Apart from consummations of this sort, however, there are others that art yields through its referential content and that science has virtually no capacity to emulate. In turning away from factuality as much as it does, art acquires a unique ability to express feelings, emotions, and even ideas that tell us about our condition as human beings. By their self-imposed constraints, abstract music, painting, sculpture are disqualified from making realistic representations of the world. Far from being calamitous, this allows them to express and therefore bring to view much that cannot be included in even the most accomplished of literal representations.

At the risk of oversimplifying what is so complex, I suggest that we can learn more about the uplifting joy of humanitarian enthusiasm from Beethoven's Third and Ninth Symphonies than from any scientific description of this experience. The same applies to the sense of longing and ultimate isolation that pervades most of the symphonies of Mahler, and of terror about life dwindling toward nothingness in the last moments of his Ninth. If one wishes to understand the feeling of inner chaos, one need only look at the paintings of Jackson Pollock. In the abstract solidity of Henry Moore's curvaceous statues, we may perceive a peace that we can possibly reach, despite our pervasive restlessness, by accepting the fact that hard, intransigent matter is the core of our humanity. These creators instill consummatory awareness that no wholly realistic representation could equal. The masters in every art do the same.

There is a school of thought, which I have discussed in another place and need not reconsider here at any length, that restricts the honorific term *aesthetic* to the formal properties of a work of art, to the form itself as it organizes relevant materials. Some writers have even insisted that since referential content takes us beyond form and matter it must be avoided in art that is truly aesthetic. Others have made the more modest claim that referential content does not have to be excluded from the art object but must always be subordinate to form and matter.

This dogmatism seems counterintuitive and quite arbitrary. Abstraction in art requires no such theories in order to justify its existence. There are different kinds of art, and many varieties of consummation that art can yield. Millions of people have enjoyed artworks because of what they said about the world through representation and expressiveness. We have no reason to deny that these referential elements carry out a legitimate, typically artistic, function. They belong to the aesthetic experience of even the most discriminating observers, and they afford consummatory values that are indigenous to the works of art that employ them.

At the same time there is an important insight that the view I am criticizing does contain, even though it misunderstands it. Much of the enjoyment we get from referential content derives from the *way in which* realistic phenomena are represented or expressed. That is what makes the difference between a prosaic statement and one that has artistic merit. Language that provides nothing but information is neither poetry nor beautiful prose. It acquires aesthetic value and becomes art only if it quickens our imagination by conveying its message through vivid and reverberating artifacts. Great poetry does that all the time. It thereby strengthens, not eliminates, the representational and expressive properties of language. Without losing its ability to tell us about the world, it communicates in a way that is both artistic and wholly suited to its medium.

This capacity of poetry, and of all the arts, including the most abstract, manifests a formal property that is ignored by those who believe in art for art's sake or any other puristic doctrine in aesthetics. Once we recognize the authenticity of enjoying how a work performs its appointed referential service, we realize that our consummatory experience in this regard is aesthetically as valid as any other. We may agree that form is paramount in art, but we will then go on to distinguish *referential* form, which guides and manages our expression or representation of reality, from the form that merely organizes materials. Like all form, both types shape and pattern, but only referential form shapes and patterns the relationship be-tween, on the one hand, the materials already structured by a work's inner form and, on the other, the reality outside that is represented or expressed by whatever referential meaning the artist gives it.

❄

This last type of consummation reveals how art can have a truthful-ness that does not occur in science or literal knowledge of the usual sort. When philosophers discuss the nature of artistic or aesthetic truth, they generally begin by remarking that in an "obvious" sense art cannot be either true or false. Imagine someone in a museum gallery going up to a work of abstract expressionism and saying as he shakes his head: "False!" How can this utterance have any mean-ing? On the surface, at least, the painting is making no assertions. The situation is totally different from the one in which a signpost indicating the location of the restrooms has been turned around in the opposite direction. Having searched in vain, a person might very well return to the signpost and correctly mutter: "False!" An explicit proposition had been made, and it was false though pur-porting to be true. Nothing of the sort applies in relation to an abstract painting.

How then can works of art, even pure abstractions, be not only true or false but *aesthetically* and *artistically* true or false? Thinkers such as Zola, in the book to which I referred, argue for what is sometimes called the "correspondence theory" of aesthetic truth. On this view works of art acquire truthfulness by presenting or duplicating reality in a manner that is analogous to factual accounts employed by descriptive science or history or journalism.

This theory is enticing inasmuch as it asserts that for anything to be true it must somehow refer to the world outside itself, the world as it actually exists. Even in an abstract painting composed of nothing but lines and colors, one might detect a truthfulness not present in any explicit proposition and yet such as to make this work of art an authentic expression of feelings or ideas about some ex-ternal reality. The Jackson Pollocks I mentioned earlier are not *just* chaotic. They also reveal the chaos in Pollock's life, and in the reality to which he belonged. Perhaps that is what Pollock meant when he said, "I am nature." Abstract paintings do not state anything overtly, since their referential content is nonrepresentational, but—however subtly—they can signify a great deal about the world at large by virtue of their expressiveness.

The correspondence theory is nevertheless confused. It naively assumes that artistic truth must always emulate the factuality paradigmatic of science, history, and journalism. But that would fail to explain the nature of abstraction, whether in painting or music or sculpture, and it would ignore crucial differences between artistic and factual truth. Even when works of art achieve their kind of truthfulness through explicit representations—as in portraits of real people or paintings of an actual event or landscapes of a known locale—they rarely offer a one-to-one correspondence to any prior facts. Not only is the artist free to rearrange reality, but also he is empowered by his medium to select from the scene before him whatever lends itself to representation in his particular art form. His work may often correspond to what exists, but never completely and never to existence in all its details.

Moreover, the truthfulness in art is basically subjective. Though the artist may wish to remain faithful to the original, his production will be aesthetically interesting only if his style, his perceptiveness, his manner of presentation express his own personality or point of view. None of this depends on literal correspondence. If one could *truly* copy reality, clone and replicate it, the correspondence theory might be defensible. But no such possibility exists, and there is no reason to think that artistic truth requires anything like it.

What has been called the "coherence theory" reacts against the shortcomings of the correspondence theory by locating truthfulness in a sense of inner rightness or necessity that art may generate in someone who responds appropriately to it. On this view artistic truth depends not on correspondence to reality but rather on the work's ability to create in its audience an attitude that is internally consistent and harmoniously integrated within itself. If *King Lear* were given a happy ending, that would be considered untruthful simply because it is incongruous with the feelings that the play arouses in us from the beginning. Although scientific truth involves correspondence to reality, it is held, artistic truth is entirely a function of coherence in the audience's response.

But this, too, is strange. Without the external thrust built into the notion of correspondence, how can an aesthetic claim to truth make any sense at all? The coherence theory may possibly explain why artworks are engrossing and even cathartic, but it hardly accounts for their being true. However much one might experience an inner rightness and harmonious unity of feeling in well-constructed detective stories, or even crossword puzzles, their aesthetic truthfulness is usually insignificant and often nonexistent.

In an attempt to avoid the difficulties of both the correspondence and the coherence theories, the "essence theory" defines aesthetic truth as a work's ability to present some essence of reality perceived through art. The essence is a universal rather than a particular. It reveals what a certain kind of entity is like and therefore portrays the nature of a genus, even when it depicts a person or a thing that belongs to that genus. According to the essence theory, artistic truth tells us about generic conditions more fundamental than their instantiations in particularities. Since art is inherently artificial and usually fictional, its transcendence of literal truths is thought to exhibit deeper verities. In this vein Aristotle said that tragedy is more "philosophical" than history, and Balzac remarked that Molière's *L'Avare* is a profound statement not about misers but about miserliness.

A critique of the essence theory would exceed the limits of this book. Nevertheless, for the purposes at hand, this approach may well prove useful in some degree. I have been discussing the nature of aesthetic truth as a means of exploring the spiritual implications in art. The correspondence and coherence theories cannot take us very far in that direction; but since the essence theory recognizes that art can be supremely philosophical, this approach might appear to be more promising. To see why it is not, we must recognize that existence is a composite of particularities, not universals, even though our conception of relevant universals may help us understand the nature of the particulars that can be subsumed within them.

In science and in ordinary life we tend to ignore this fact, since the difference between one particular and another is often unimportant for practical purposes. If we take a random sample of coffee beans in order to reach an inductive conclusion about the ripeness of the contents in a shipment, it does not matter which are the individual beans we choose. For the accurate generalization we are trying to make, all instances are equally good. To ask about the condition of some particular coffee bean would be to take a different kind of attitude. But it is precisely this alternate approach that distinguishes aesthetic truthfulness from scientific truth. The two may be compatible with each other, and frequently they are. In its emphasis on universals, however, the essence theory confounds the two.

Aristotle and Balzac are therefore mistaken in the aphorisms I have cited. Balzac is wrong to think that anyone would cherish *L'Avare* if Harpagon were only the personification of miserliness. Regardless of how well he typifies the universal that enables us to identify this salient trait of his, no human being can be reduced to that or any other attribute. We are all a unity of many traits. We place our individual stamp on them, and our character, our behavior, our supervening mentality mold them into a configuration that is our personal identity. If Harpagon were just the embodiment of miserliness, he would have none of the humanity that makes him as ridiculous and as pathetic as he is. Molière wanted him to be an object of fun, a man who is absurd in his relation to money as well as to other people. The play succeeds, to the extent that it does, because Molière portrays Harpagon as a particular person like many we may know, and sufficiently resembling them to make us laugh at any of these individuals.

In the case of Aristotle the fundamental error is classificatory, in the sense that his statement relies on a preconception about what shall count as philosophy or history. Saying that tragedy is more philosophical than history, Aristotle would seem to limit history to the giving of factual data about the past—what this or that person did or said on this or that occasion. And, of course, he is right about *some* histories, for instance chronicles. But other works of history, including Thucydides', which Aristotle had in mind, provide a sense of the moment-by-moment evolution of events that have a trajectory peculiar to themselves. If a historian can convey the uniqueness of these temporal realities, his or her writing will be just as philosophical in the realm of the actual as the tragedian's is in the realm of the imaginary. The essence theory fails to account for this.

In making these comments about aesthetic truth, I am proposing an approach that has often been neglected. Without engaging in technical disputes about universals and particulars, I need only cite Schopenhauer's belief that in the order of nature all individuals are merely exemplifications of their species, which is itself nothing but a manifestation of the unitary force that flows dynamically through existence as a whole. Schopenhauer claims that two leaves on the branch of a tree are really one and the same, not only because they look identical but also because they are indistinguishable products of the same ultimate reality.

This view of individuals runs counter to everything I believe, and therefore to the radical pluralism that is foundational to all the suggestions I have made. If Schopenhauer's intuition is more acceptable to the reader than mine is, that person will find no merit in my ideas about aesthetic truth. They are predicated on the belief that the particularity of every entity is irreducible in itself, and that art achieves its type of truthfulness by showing how each individual is uniquely what it is. Aesthetic truth, as opposed to scientific or other kinds of truth, defeats the project of essentialism. It displays the difference and diversity there is in all existence, if only because everything is delimited by its own space and time. Much more is involved in this than one might imagine. Disparity in spatial and temporal coordinates propagates other differences as well. That is a reality we cannot escape.

Some of what I am now stating may sound familiar to those who have read prequels to this book, above all in the places where I describe love as an acceptance of the indefeasible uniqueness in whatever receives our affective interest. That idea is central to the concept of bestowal, which I have defined as a necessary condition for love to exist. The spirituality of art pertains to its ability to focus one's attention, and possibly one's admiration, upon the particularity of some being. Various philosophers have thought we attain, through love, truths about the beloved that we could not have acquired unless we loved him or her. As a theory of love, this view may not be defensible. But it becomes more plausible as a characterization of artistic truth. The kind of truthfulness that art provides results from a bestowal approximating love, the artist having given extraordinary importance to what distinguishes the particular aesthetic object from everything else. The effort consists in probing into specific attributes of a thing or person or ideal. When this creative act is carried out with superlative talent as well as depth of mind and soul, it issues into a work that is aesthetically true to life.

Art and love are therefore companions within the realm of spirit. Both are dedicated to the maximizing of consummation, and each enables the other to reach its own spirituality. We recognize as much when we applaud those happy few who successfully practice the art of love, and when we admire connoisseurs who enjoy the love of art.

Art is not loved for its truthfulness alone, of course, for it also yields other types of consummation—through its inherent form and satisfying materials as well as through different aspects of its referential meaning. Nevertheless, it is because artistic truth puts us in touch with reality, and transcends the merely factual, that all great art has about it an aura of nobility and even sanctity. In his song *An die Musik*, Schubert both expresses and fulfills his devotion to music. He thanks it for having kindled in his heart the warmth of love. He calls it a "noble art." This is proper and wonderfully moving, since Schubert worshiped music as a source of consummation and of meaning in his life. But every other art is equally noble, equally indicative of how nature improves itself through imagination and idealization. Art *is* the spirituality of nature. And since there is no spirit apart from nature, only by reference to art can we explain the spirituality in ethics or religion. All art seeks to harmonize meaning and happiness; but if it attains aesthetic truthfulness, it achieves a further harmony. Its bestowal of value is then an act of love that creates something new and possibly beautiful while also revealing the character of nature's own creativity. Can spirit rise higher than that?

9

THE CONTINUUM
OF ENDS & MEANS

❦

In Chapter 1 I suggested that Schopenhauer's disbelief about positive happiness fails to account for the harmonious organization of experience which exists in an ends-means continuum. This concept permeates the writings of John Dewey, filling them with practical wisdom about the creative and healthy-minded existence to which human beings have access under socially optimal conditions.

Dewey realizes, as much as Schopenhauer does, that a hostile environment can always crush human hopes of happiness. But unlike Schopenhauer, he encourages us to face all natural hardships with the pragmatist faith that often, at least, we can work out an acceptable accommodation under the circumstances. Dewey sees our world as an organic interweave of valued experience and impersonal physical necessity. In its own internal configuration his philosophy is also highly unified. His conception of the ends-means continuum appears not only in his aesthetics but also in his ethical theory and throughout his writings on the good life. It is an idea that fructifies his speculation at many points. Throughout this chapter I will try to extend its implications beyond the borders of Dewey's philosophy, but always contiguous with them.

❋

As the basis of his analysis, Dewey distinguishes between "prizing" and "appraising." Although I have been influenced by Dewey, my own distinction between bestowal and appraisal addresses valuational questions in a somewhat different way. In a later chapter I explain why this is so. Dewey's distinction is crucial to his theory because he wants to argue that nothing can be established as truly valuable apart from processes of deliberation and adjudication which he calls "intelligence." To that extent, valuation requires an act of appraising. For something to be truly valuable, intelligent reflection must find it justifiable under the conditions in which it occurs. On the other hand, everything that is actually prized by someone can be a candidate for validation of this sort. What Dewey means by the word *prizing* is not entirely clear. At times he associates prizing with wanting, desiring, holding dear, caring about, and similar manifestations of human interest; but occasionally he sounds as if attending *to* and taking care *of* might also belong to the attitude he has in mind.

In his usual fashion, Dewey seeks to overcome an erroneous dualism, in this case between prizing and appraising separated from each other and used as the bases of different theories of value. Both are needed for something to have authentic worth, Dewey insists, and each must function in a permanent interaction with the other. He therefore rejects the hedonist's reliance on pleasure as an ultimate value. An immediate enjoyment, one that occurs gratuitously and is generally prized by the person who experiences it, may or may not be valuable. That must be determined by an act of appraisal, which considers the consequences of this experience, its cost, either to oneself or others, and the means by which it was procured. Even when pleasure or enjoyment is the goal one seeks, Dewey denies that it can have the ultimacy that hedonists and many utilitarians have accorded it. He claims that nothing can be an "end-in-itself," since the value of any end must be gauged only in relation to the means that bring it into being and the practical sequelae to which it leads.

As a substitute for traditional thinking about ends-in-themselves, Dewey introduces the concept of "end-in-view." Anything that someone seeks as a desirable possibility is an end-in-view, but only if it issues from appraising as well as prizing. It is foreseen both as an attainment that will satisfy one's needs or inclinations and as the embodiment of means that one must use in order to procure it. Ends-in-view that Dewey considers truly valuable are always continuous with the means that bring them into being. These are not separable. The means are themselves ends-in-view. They interpenetrate the goal that is being sought, and their own value or disvalue inevitably affects one's appraisal of that goal. As Dewey puts it: "Every condition that has to be brought into existence in order to serve as means is, *in that connection*, an object of desire and an end-in-view, while the end actually reached is a means to future ends as well as a test of valuations previously made."[1]

In saying this, Dewey suggests that value is always relevant to an organic continuum that escapes any essentialistic dualism between means and ends. The usual distinction between "instrumental goods" and "intrinsic goods" he finds untenable because an instrumentality is itself an end-in-view one has chosen as a means to a desired end, while that particular end leads on to other eventualities for which it too is instrumental. Nothing has value apart from this continuum of means that are also ends-in-view and ends-in-view that are also means. As a result, there cannot be any intrinsic goods that are wholly distinct from the instrumental goods that make them possible.

Various consequences of Dewey's theory are worth exploring. But first, we should put it in the context of ideas in the history of philosophy that pertain to the subject matter of this book. To begin with, it completely rejects the point of view that Aristotle articulates in the *Politics* as follows: "When there is one thing that is means and another that is end, there is *nothing common* between them, except in so far as the one, the means, produces, and the other, the end, receives the product."[2] This conception, which Dewey rightly sees as the basis for class stratification in society, splits human experience into two insuperable modalities: one in which people do various things that are inherently valueless and even repellent though necessary as the means of getting what they want; the other in which they have a consummatory experience that leads nowhere, since it is presumed to be complete in itself. In a nondemocratic state such as the polis Aristotle idealizes, different individuals belong either to a subordinate class that provides servile benefits to others, or else to a favored elite that acquires the final goods of life without being concerned about instrumentalities required for them to occur.

On Dewey's view, this political arrangement is morally unacceptable. In a good society, he insists, all activities, and all persons who either enjoy life or make enjoyment possible, derive whatever value they have only through the continuum of ends and means. Commendable actions are alike in being means that are also ends-in-view and ends-in-view that are themselves means to further ends, each culmination in the ongoing search for goodness being constituted by the instrumentalities that precede it.

Dewey's conception of value runs counter to the one enunciated by Hume, who was following Aristotle in this matter. In his attempt to show that the "ultimate ends of human actions" cannot depend upon our rational faculties alone, Hume claims that all deliberation about value terminates in "sentiments and affections" that are accepted as finalities. Our reasoning would go on forever, Hume maintains, unless we recognized that "something must be desirable on its own account."[3]

To my way of thinking, Dewey's approach is preferable to Aristotle's and Hume's. In ruling out the possibility of any final or intrinsic end-in-itself, Dewey enables us to explain value in a strictly empirical manner. He precludes the existence of an end that can be justified a priori, apart from its relations to both causes and their consequences. Earlier events that lead up to what is valued, and later events that issue from it, are all integral to its goodness. Dewey's view is relativistic inasmuch as it recognizes no *summum bonum* that could serve as a universal or irrefutable standard. The good life arises from the efforts of creatures in nature who prize some affective outcome but have to appraise its desirability or perniciousness within the complex of realities that are always present and problematic. Without behavior of this sort, nothing can be valuable and life itself cannot continue. I read somewhere of Dewey telling an interviewer that life is like climbing a range of mountain peaks, and that once a person has reached the top of one mountain he or she must then move on to others in the range. When his interviewer asked what happens if there are no peaks left, Dewey calmly replied: "You die."

Even though Dewey's philosophy recognizes no ultimate standards of value that determine in advance what can or cannot be good, it nevertheless provides a naturalistic account of justifiable valuations. All values originate from a state of lack or need or malfunctioning that an organism undergoes in the time, space, and other coordinates that constitute its daily existence. Seeking to rectify its condition of deprivation, Dewey says, the organism engages in appetitive behavior directed toward some end-in-view. If its effort is successful, it will experience a consummation that eliminates the initial discomfort and becomes a value that it may seek through later attempts to survive and to flourish in its natural setting.

Individual, and specific, consummation is therefore the ultimate goal of any putative value. But since every consummation is always subject to appraisal of its cost and consequences, each instance must belong to a continuum of ends and means in order to establish itself as valuable. A consummation that is authentically good serves as a means to further consummations while also being in itself an end-in-view that includes whatever means have contributed to its own occurrence. Consummations that exist as ends in detachment from past or future means—as in the case of fantasies, daydreams, hopes out of context, or lunacies both normal and pathological—do not reveal the nature of value but are merely simulations of it.

❄

To the extent that Dewey's philosophy is founded on these ideas about the continuum of ends and means, it is not *wholly* relativistic. On the contrary, it ordains criteria that supersede any momentary whim or wish fulfillment. Within their naturalistic framework, Deweyan appraisal and intelligence are quasi-objective methods for establishing what may or may not be good for men and women functioning in everyday life as conditions necessitate. The cognitive elements of valuation are the same as, or quite similar to, those that pertain to scientific investigations of every sort. When Dewey argues, as he frequently does, that morality must be dealt with scientifically, he does so in the hope that the great achievements in physical and biological science can be duplicated by a comparable methodology in morals.

Using the continuum of ends and means as the model for determining what is or is not valuable, Dewey appeals to health and healthy-minded existence as the ultimate standard for the good life. That is a major achievement of his philosophy. Yet those who believe that life in this world is but a prelude to a better one that spirit craves may find his approach stultifying to their aspirations. They must also wonder about various internal problems that beset Dewey's scientistic views. For instance, if the continuum of ends and means discloses the character of authentic valuation, what is the grounding for either this continuum or valuation itself? Religious writers have always known that the "temporal world" can afford gratifications and fulfillments that are alluring to creatures like us, but they generally wished to contrast mere organic well-being with superior goods the enlightened spirit can obtain only by detaching itself from nature or, at least, trying to rise above it.

Dewey has nothing to say about metaphysical possibilities of this sort, and neither have I. But unlike Dewey, I sympathize with those who feel that naturalistic conceptions such as ours are somehow lacking. Instead of dismissing transcendentalist intimations as summarily as Dewey does, I want to examine more thoroughly than he, and from a slightly different point of view, the imagination that goes into them. That attempt occurs later in this book.

In this place I merely reiterate my belief that naturalism espoused by Dewey, as well as by myself, is also a metaphysical view. Although prizing, appraising, intelligence, and the continuum of ends and means refer to empirical realities, there can be no empirical assurance, no way of proving, that they reveal the nature of what is truly valuable. To use the idea of health and organic success as substantiation would be to argue in a circle. Accepting these or comparable coordinates as fundamental criteria, we voice a credo that is as unverifiable as the ones that orthodox believers prefer. Once we recognize that imagination is a controlling factor in either type of affirmation, however, we may no longer feel embarrassed by this similitude.

There are other problematic aspects of Dewey's philosophy. His outlook is pervasively democratic in the sense that every consummation that receives the approval of appraisal and intelligence is treated equally as a human value. Since they supplant any final standards of valuation that might exist apart from the egalitarian and unbiased functioning of the ends-means continuum, appraisal and intelligence are themselves democratic. No inherited, conventional, or rigidly dogmatic priorities are to hold sway within the continuum; until proven otherwise, each desire or inclination must be considered an innocent candidate for value. But, we may ask, what justifies making democracy the ultimate ground for valuation? Once again, Dewey's thought would seem to be engaged in a circularity.[4]

All the same, these difficulties need not deter us from acknowledging that Dewey's vision is beneficial. His ideas about the valuational continuum point the way not only to an adequate conception of happiness but also to a fertile account of how aesthetic, ethical, and religious attitudes can each be understood from a naturalistic point of view.

❊

Though Dewey does not, to my knowledge, discuss Schopenhauer's argument about the pendulum of life that makes happiness impossible, his entire philosophy is clearly inimical to any such approach. Schopenhauer's analysis is predicated upon the kind of dualism between desire and satisfaction that Dewey rejects. If wanting something and finally getting it are linked within a continuum of ends and means, happiness becomes a viable positivity in a way that Schopenhauer does not recognize. For the wanting or desiring is then seen to be an instance of prizing that must be appraised in accordance with means of gratification that become ends-in-view we care about. As such, both ends and means are not only meaningful to us but also integrated components within a natural process that creates happiness through its own momentum. Getting what we want can scarcely eventuate in boredom if the achieved goal is, at one and the same time, both the end we sought in order to gratify our desire and a means leading on to further ends that exist as extensions of the same continuum. As long as life persists in this manner, Dewey would say, there is no pendulum that could swing between deprivation and an alternate state of ennui.

I think Dewey is right in suggesting that human beings can hope for real happiness to the extent that their experience consists of an ongoing continuum between ends and means, and like him I see nothing in the striving of organic beings to prevent this from happening under favorable circumstances. I nevertheless have qualms about Dewey's muscular pragmatism, much as Santayana felt uneasy about William James's melioristic heartiness and will to believe that the world can always be changed for the better. Both James and Dewey realized that in time there would be no time, that the earth, the sun, and everything we designate as the universe will disappear and leave not a rack behind. But, in their eagerness to get humanity involved in healthy and productive behavior, they seemed to underplay this aspect of their pervasive naturalism. Schopenhauer may have been somewhat neurotic in his emphasis upon the fact of universal suffering, but Santayana applauded his trenchant refusal to ignore dire conditions that limit the ability of mortals to be authentically happy for very long. I, too, admire him for that.

Schopenhauer's pessimism about happiness culminated in his ideas of compassion and the salvation available to us through identification with fellow sufferers in the universe. These ideas need to be discussed separately. But in the meantime I want to remark that Dewey's buoyant activism may be a more reliable guide to the nature of compassion than Schopenhauer's negativism. Dewey shows us not only the logic of conduct that is both purposive and inherently valuable but also the practical workings of intelligence and scientific inquiry needed for compassion to have its greatest effect in the merciless and basically unfeeling domain of physical reality. In contrast to Dewey's concern for *what must be done*, Schopenhauer's views about compassion as an ethical attitude seem mystical and largely cerebral.

What, then, is the flaw in Dewey's conception of happiness as a possible product of the ends-means continuum? I detect it in a passage in which Dewey talks about the psychological setting of the continuum, arising as it does out of desires that manifest a lack or need of some sort. He says that

> desires arise only when "there is something the matter," when there is some "trouble" in an existing situation. When analyzed, this "something the matter" is found to spring from the fact that there is something lacking, wanting, in the existing situation as it stands, an absence which produces conflict in the elements that do exist. When things are going completely smoothly, desires do not arise, and there is no occasion to project ends-in-view, for "going smoothly" signifies that there is no need for effort and struggle. It suffices to let things take their "natural" course.[5]

But what are we being asked to contemplate? A world in which things can sometimes go completely smoothly, in which there are occasions when effort and struggle are not at all needed? Things are said to take their natural course under these circumstances, and neither desires nor ends-in-view would then come into being. But no such reality exists. If Dewey believes otherwise, he reveals that his system of thought has not been fully purged of its original idealism. The great virtue of Schopenhauer's pessimism is its unswerving realization that life is *always* a process of struggle, of effort, of competition for survival. Desires and the goals that may possibly satisfy them are the offshoots of unending restlessness fundamental to the very nature of animate existence. *That* is the natural course of things for living entities, as Dewey himself should have recognized in view of the anecdote about successive mountains to be scaled.

One might say that there is only a trivial difference between

Dewey's and Schopenhauer's thinking about the origin of desires, since Dewey admits that usually something is the matter and so action must be taken. As I have mentioned, his activism is more pervasive and concerted than Schopenhauer's. Nevertheless, their divergent attitudes toward the world in which one acts create a chasm between their philosophies. Compared with Schopenhauer, Dewey sounds forever cheerful and serene about the consummations that can eventuate from our struggles with nature. Although he never depicts an actual situation in which everything, or anything, runs so smoothly that further efforts and desires do not occur, he seems to assume that each moment of consummation provides a symbolic replica of what that utopian condition might be. Schopenhauer reviles the notion that this or any other type of total peace and quiescence can be found in nature. The paths of salvation may enable us to achieve a valued freedom from desire, Schopenhauer says, but only because they involve a systematic repudiation of nature itself.

Although possibly less hardheaded and realistic than Schopenhauer, Dewey offers an outlook that is more wholesome and more balanced in its naturalism. It shows awareness of the benign potentialities in life without being simpleminded about nature's destructiveness and basic indifference toward human welfare. Dewey's philosophy is never embittered about reality, as Schopenhauer's often is. What I find missing in Dewey is a sense of horror or indignation about the suffering (by other entities, if not oneself) that underlies whatever consummations the happy and well-constituted activist may experience as he or she goes on successfully harmonizing ends and means. Dewey thinks of nature as an ally in its own domestication. Would he have this massive faith if he focused on its terrifying aspects as relentlessly as Schopenhauer does?

Faith that combines the perspectives of both Schopenhauer and a pragmatist like Dewey is what Nietzsche tried to depict in his notion of *amor fati*. Before discussing that, however, we should consider the way that Dewey's ideas about the continuum of ends and means enriched his use of utilitarian concepts of happiness. Dewey begins by distinguishing what he calls the "subjective side" of happiness from its objective conditions. He rejects traditional hedonism because it identifies happiness with the experience of pleasure, either in a momentary occurrence or in the summation of a lifetime, thereby ignoring the external circumstances that are required for pleasure to exist. According to Dewey, even to search for pleasure presupposes an attempt to change the environment to one's own advantage. That or any comparable activity will succeed in creating happiness, he maintains, only if the steps one takes are interwoven with the desired outcome. The subjective and the objective attitudes must therefore be fused, as they are when a continuum of ends and means pervades our pursuit of the good things in life.

Insofar as hedonism neglects the objective, Dewey states, it misconstrues the nature of happiness. But he commends the utilitarianism of John Stuart Mill, since it recognizes not only that personal and social interests are intermeshed but also that happiness consists of more than just the greatest quantity of pleasure. He also credits Mill with having perceived the underlying paradox in earlier versions of hedonism: "As long as a man seeks for happiness he will not get it. But if he stops thinking about it and devotes himself to certain objective interests, the pursuit of science, art, industry, then the happiness will come."[6]

Dewey's conception of the ends-means continuum as a prerequisite for happiness is therefore wholly compatible with Mill's philosophy. Dewey uses language that makes fewer references to pleasure than Mill does, but his emphasis upon value as the fulfillment of desires that are acceptable in view of their consequences and their cost can be read as a supplement to Mill's idealization of pleasures that are qualitatively of the highest order. For Dewey as for Mill, these higher pleasures are to be found in aesthetic as well as moral experience, both of which are considered cognitively harmonious with scientific investigation. The distance between Mill and Dewey is not very great.

✳

In *Art as Experience* Dewey applies his reasoning about the continuum of ends and means to various problems in aesthetics. In one place he distinguishes between "*mere* means" and the kind that "is taken up into the consequences produced and remains immanent in them."[7] The former are separate from the ends they help to establish; they are absent in the final product, though possibly essential for it to exist. The latter means play a role in what they bring about, much as bricks and mortar are a part of a building and not just the means by which it is constructed. When we talk about an artistic medium, Dewey remarks, we are referring to means not only employed in a particular art form but also definitive of it. "Colors *are* the painting; tones are the music. . . . Esthetic effects belong intrinsically to their medium; when another medium is substituted, we have a stunt rather than an object of art."[8]

Dewey suggests a similar distinction with respect to ends. Whether it is the goal of some artwork to represent reality, or to convey a message, or to explore technical possibilities in the medium, it will not be aesthetic unless its colors, tones, words, and other elements have intrinsic and constitutive importance within the specific ends to which the project is devoted. When that happens, "means and end coalesce."[9] Citing a remark the painter Delacroix made, Dewey says that depicting objects through color is aesthetic but coloration is not. It is one thing to apply colors *to* objects in the representation and another to make the objects *out of* colors.

Though Dewey formulates these valuational ideas in the course of his aesthetic analysis, they clearly extend beyond the limits of what is ordinarily known as art. For if the coalescence of ends and means constitutes the aesthetic, and if the aesthetic is defined as the consummatory aspect of experience, then all of life can be considered potentially aesthetic and a source of consummation when structured in accordance with the ends-means continuum. No one before Dewey had developed this conception as thoroughly and as persuasively as he did. Its utility for humanistic philosophy of the type that I have been exploring is enormous.

For one thing, it enables us to interpret the entire field of values from an aesthetic point of view. In the chapters that immediately preceded this one, I suggested that art is humankind's supreme device for harmonizing happiness and meaning, and that everything in life that effects this harmonization may count as art. If we now approach valuation in terms of the continuum of ends and means, and then specify that whenever this unity issues into consummatory experience it reveals artistic achievement at its best, we will have identified the good life with life as a work of art. The aesthetic may then be considered foundational to all value, wherever and however it occurs.

That is, in fact, what I believe. Though this view has been presented in its abstract outlines and needs more analysis, it can help us in our attempt to harmonize concepts of nature and spirit. Dewey perceives this too. Explaining his ideas about ends and means being fused in art, he frequently relies on examples that are drawn from ethics and from religion as seen from a naturalistic perspective. A paragraph in *Art as Experience* encapsulates the vision that appears in all his voluminous writing:

> Being "good" for the sake of avoiding penalty, whether it be going to jail or to hell, makes conduct unlovely. It is as anesthetic as is going to the dentist's chair so as to avoid a lasting injury. When the Greeks identified the good and beautiful in actions, they revealed, in their feeling of grace and proportion in right conduct, a perception of fusion of means and ends. . . . In all ranges of experience, externality of means defines the mechanical. Much of what is termed spiritual is also unesthetic. But the unesthetic quality is because the things denoted by the word also exemplify separation of means and end; the "ideal" is so cut off from the realities, by which alone it can be striven for, that it is vapid. The "spiritual" gets a local habitation and achieves the solidity of form required for esthetic quality only when it is embodied in a sense of actual things. Even angels have to be provided in imagination with bodies and wings.[10]

Inspiring as these words are, they still raise questions and leave room for amplification. What is the relation between aesthetic imagination and the living of an ethical or spiritual life? How do the ethical and the spiritual differ? How can they be harmonized? If ends and means may be fused in either or in both, what is the individual continuum that defines each of them? These are the matters for which we must now seek a resolution.

AESTHETIC
FOUNDATIONS OF ETHICS
& RELIGION

🌿

The continuum of ends and means has special importance in understanding the nature of aesthetic experience. But since the aesthetic is foundational to all values, insofar as it manifests the imagination creating consummatory possibilities, its reliance upon harmonious unity between ends and means can also help us to resolve problems in the fields of ethics and religion. The tendency to separate ends and means has its origins in dualistic presuppositions that pervade most ethical and religious thinking in the West. Although the Greeks spoke of the good and the beautiful as if they were really one, Plato's distinction between appearance and reality relegated all mundane values to the merely useful in life while revering the final ends that only deductive reason could disclose. The good and the beautiful might inhere in both realms, but they could not be attained in their purity until we cleansed ourselves of our love for the seductive and inevitably extraneous instrumentalities of this world. It was thought that ethical and religious truth would put us in touch with an ideal reality that transcends the aesthetic.

Even Schopenhauer, who extolled the aesthetic as a path of salvation that defeats our bondage to the will, believed that art can provide this spiritual service only by turning away from all that is useful for preserving and prolonging life. The useful is an agency of the will; but, according to Schopenhauer, art helps us to emancipate ourselves from the will. It does so by creating something—abstract music, for instance—that has no utility whatsoever. In Santayana's philosophy, similar ideas structure his distinction between arts that are "servile" and those that are "fine." While the former have instrumental value, as in the many activities that prepare us for the enjoyment of life, the latter are said to acquaint us with the ends that truly represent ethical and religious values. These can occur at any moment in life and in any empirical setting; but they belong to a different realm of being.

Difficulties in Santayana's approach emanate from his thoughts about the ontology of spirit, to which I will presently return. Nevertheless, in his own way, Santayana also tries to overcome some of the traditional dualisms that occur in the history of aesthetic philosophy. In the eighteenth century many theorists—Dr. Johnson, for instance—claimed that great art must be didactic, inculcating moral truths and emulating philosophy and religion in its depiction of "general nature." In the nineteenth century this conception was attacked by proponents of art for art's sake. They held that art need not adhere to any of the standards that pertain to ethics, philosophy, or religion. On the contrary, they identified the aesthetic with consummatory experience, either of materials or of forms that organize materials into an autotelic whole, and whether or not the work of art contains an ethical message or religious outlook. In his writings on art and the aesthetic, Santayana sought to harmonize the contrary notions, thus defeating this particular dualism.

Like those who believed in art for art's sake, Santayana defined the aesthetic in terms of materials and forms immediately given to the spectator apart from any referential content and regardless of whether the art object was designed to represent or express feelings and ideas about the world. But Santayana also insisted that this was only a minimal requirement for artistic excellence. A work would have greater value *as art*, he thought, if it also conveyed moral and quasi-religious insights that gave it philosophical scope coherent with the beauty provided by its form and materials. In effect, Dewey held a similar view about art; nor is Santayana's aesthetics wholly inconsistent with Dewey's ideas about the continuum of ends and means. As against the thinking of Tolstoy, for instance, they both rejected the dogma that art should devote itself to the furthering of didactic ends. As against formalists such as Clive Bell or Roger Fry, however, Santayana and Dewey denied that referential content was intrinsically nonaesthetic.

Parallel to the ideational split between art and ethics or religion, there also existed throughout the Western tradition a split between ethics and religion. It is most vividly presented in Sophocles' *Antigone*. The drama in that play issues from the fact that Creon's decree forbidding the burial of Polyneices is sanctioned by a standard of moral and political action that the audience would consider entirely legitimate. In defying Creon's orders, Antigone knowingly violates the ethical code in which she herself believes. She claims that obligations to her dead brother devolve from religious commandments that must be given priority over the merely ethical. In his sensitivity to the pity and terror of the human situation, Sophocles depicts the chasm between ethical and religious attitudes that may be sundered from each other at any time. But he does not indicate how they can be joined or reconciled.

In Christian theology systematic attempts were made to eliminate the possibility of a conflict between ethics and religion. Each was defined in terms of the same progenitor, God, who created everything with a moral intent articulated in his revealed mandates. Nevertheless, the controversies between the secular and the ecclesiastic, between state and church, between conscience and devotion, between the good and the holy—in other words, between ethics and religion—manifest a division that pervaded the prevalent ideology and affected daily decision making.

I can readily illustrate this insidious bifurcation of thought by mentioning two fundamental problems in Christian theology. First, there is the question about God's being. In Christianity, God is identified with love. Together with whatever else that means, which I have discussed in other books, God is considered to be all-loving. He bestows goodness indiscriminately upon everything that exists, regardless of its merit and whether or not it is good or evil. Yet God is also described as a lawgiver and judge who on the final day will separate the good from the evil, consigning the latter to everlasting perdition while the former glow eternally in the sanctity of his luminous being.

The second problem is related to the first one but shows more directly how hard it is for devout believers to follow the spiritual life they have chosen as their mission. In the Bible human beings are told to love others as they love themselves, to forgive wrongdoers, and even to love their enemies. Does this imply that prisons are to be emptied and criminals no longer punished? Are principles of good and evil to be ignored by one who follows the path to spirituality? Is ethics transcended for the greater glory of religion? Most Christians would answer no to questions such as these. But it is not entirely clear how this response can be justified, and throughout the centuries different efforts have been made to harmonize what persistently threaten to be divergent vectors within the doctrines of the church.

Since I have no desire to preserve a transcendental view of any sort, I will not try to unify Christian ethics and religion. To take the next step in my argument, I can demonstrate the inadequacy of the relevant dichotomy by focusing on the ontological beliefs of Santayana, who was an atheist and avowed materialist in philosophy. Santayana's lingering but powerful allegiance to his Catholic origins appears not only in his Neoplatonism but also in his conception of spirit. He depicts the spiritual aspect of human nature as the tendency in all men and women to pursue absolute truth, pure and indiscriminate love of the search for love in everything, and untrammeled contemplation of the infinite essences (quasi-Platonic forms) that constitute whatever we can imagine as a possibility for existence.

Santayana speaks of a "realm" of spirit in order to emphasize that the spiritual life cannot be reduced to any other. He shows its unique character by delineating the differences between spirit and matter. Though spirit issues out of matter, he insists that spirit is detached from worldly interests, incapable of affecting the dynamic flow of what exists, and despite its passion for knowing and loving all things that do or might exist it remains forever relegated to the condition of a spectator. Spirit, as Santayana portrays it, cannot act; it can only contemplate. Yet what it contemplates reveals essentialistic truths about the possible beauty as well as the actual tragedy in reality as a whole.

Santayana's conception of spirit seems to me radically deficient. It treats our capacity for creating and discovering values as if by definition that is separate from the physical dimensions of our being. Although Santayana recognizes, indeed insists, that spirit is always an emanation from the realm of matter and therefore subject to its causal determinants, he sees spirit as the part of conscious and reflective organisms that senses their detachment from the material order. This alienation shows itself in their consciousness, their memory, their foresight, their powers of imagination and idealization, and, above all, their ability to intuit the endless expanse of essences that are immediately given in their experience. Santayana's belief that detachment and pervasive alienation cannot be avoided by creatures like ourselves is what I find most dubious in his notion of spirit.

Saying that spirit is detached from its origins in the material complex of vital processes that control each animal at its organic level, Santayana refers to more than just the *feelings* of alienation people sometimes undergo. As human beings with the kind of consciousness that we have, Santayana claims, we are always and inherently homeless in the realm of matter. He thinks our stranded condition results from the fact that spirit is totally unable to alter anything in the flux of physical energy, which generates existence at every moment.

Santayana believes that the animal and vegetative elements of our being, which he calls "psyche," do have real, albeit limited, causal efficacy in the realm of matter. But though he considers spirit a by-product of psyche, he denies that spirit itself can influence the chain of cause and effect. It can only look and feel and imagine: it can do nothing that would make a difference in how things are. Spirit merely watches the spectacle that reality makes available to consciousness in a panorama of "free entertainment," as Santayana calls it. And since so much of reality is ruthless, harmful, and inimical to human values, spirit is pained by what appears before it. But it is unable to take action against any sea of troubles it observes.

As Santayana describes it, spirit laments not only its alienation but also the suffering of everything that lives in agony and dies ignominiously. It imagines alternate possibilities and envisages ideals that psyche may sometimes take as inspirational to its independent quest for survival and fulfillment. In itself, however, spirit is doomed, like Cassandra in Greek mythology, to the hopelessness of seeing all but changing nothing, to the martyrdom of being cut off even from those with whom it commiserates, and to the anguish of imagining the plight of innocent consummations that will be annihilated sooner or later, in one fashion or another. Santayana portrays spirit as the crucified Christ in every one of us.

In finding this conception dubious as ontology, I realize that Santayana does not limit spirit to its moments of grieving and its sense of uttermost despair. He sees that alienation can provide compensatory enjoyments. Forced to stand back from the factuality of existence, spirit can relish aesthetic and hedonic goods that would be unavailable if it took upon itself the burdens of conscientious labor and administration. In Santayana's novel *The Last Puritan*, spirit is presented under different guises in the two main characters. Puritanical Oliver is throttled in himself and in his relations to others. He personifies that much of spirit which suffers all but alters nothing as it would like. But his Latinate cousin Mario flits through life quite happily, savoring consummations that are wholly gratifying though generally superficial. Santayana's view is not problematic because it is too gloomy or negative but rather because it falsifies the way in which spirit and matter are intertwined in human nature.[1]

This harmonization, or oneness, does not extend to all animate existence. Not every creature exemplifies it. Only few occasions of life—notably, though not exclusively, in our species—manifest spirit as a fully developed phenomenon. When spirit does occur and reach its recognizable efflorescence, it exists not as an alienated disposition separate from its native psyche but as an epiphany that shows forth the possible grandeur of that psyche. Without being *reducible* to anything else, its identity is permeated with the material realities that constitute psyche. Spirit may even have survival value for the organism in which it arises. Consciousness is not a sport of nature detached from the causal mechanisms that operate in life. It is awareness of what there is that can help or injure a living creature, and it knows what makes existence worthwhile.

When it carries out this self-preservatory function efficiently and with an economy of means, conscious experience can have consummations that may seem unrelated to biological utility. And sometimes, as in the epicycles of abstract pursuits, any such use may well have become attenuated or remote. Spirit then rollicks in sheer enjoyment of itself, *as if* it were liberated from the realities that usually encase it. But despite this sense of freedom, for which spirit often hungers, it is always engulfed in the natural conditions that keep it afloat while also imposing constraints upon it. When its buds open in the spring, a rose plant may think that it is now emancipated from the soil in which its roots are embedded. Far from that being the case, its glorious offshoot is what it is not only because it gets nourishment through those roots but also because it is the revelation of what happens to them when their vitality is transformed in a way that we recognize as distinctive to rose plants. The same holds for spirit in relation to the human psyche.

Santayana's conception, like the one I am proposing, manifests a naturalistic desire to remain faithful to many of the values that were promoted by traditional nonnaturalistic doctrines while also hewing, as they did not, to the facts of material existence. But Santayana could not free himself of that much of Christianity, above all the Spanish Catholicism to which he was born, that portrays the soul of man as partly cheerful, alert, and buoyant but also as pitiful and hopelessly removed from its source in nature, isolated from ultimate power and therefore doomed to suffering permanent hardships reality has ordained for it.

A naturalism that was more fully disintoxicated from Western religion would not have encumbered its message with this perspective. In that regard, Santayana's philosophy resembles Schopenhauer's more than one might have thought. Both thinkers employ a version of the Platonic theory of forms; both consider nature an aimless field of energy, which is for them the underlying substance in everything; and both define the life of spirit as a quasi-mystical withdrawal from the bane of existence.

As an opponent of this view, I am not suggesting that nature is universally benign toward any of its creatures. Nor am I sententiously recommending the virtues of strenuous involvement in the affairs of the world. And I am certainly not suggesting that those who have these virtues will be adequately rewarded, either here or hereafter. I only wish to be more precise than Santayana or Schopenhauer in detailing the nature of value and its reliance upon imagination and idealization of the sort that is characteristic of our humanity. A truer picture of spirit, and of its dependence on nature, may then develop.

This dependence is sometimes irksome for spirit, which can feel forever alienated from its source, as children or grown citizens feel when they believe that they are not loved by their parents or by the state. But even those who react this way, and for good reason, may also intuit that the organic bond that makes the relationship so painful can simultaneously provide desired benefits as well. The mind may wish, as Hamlet's does, that this too too solid flesh would melt, thaw, and resolve itself into a dew of nothingness. But if that occurred, where would the mind be? Not in a place of its own, some ethereal tower from which it looks out upon the vastness of infinite nature, but in a void, which is to say, nowhere at all.

Though spirit may have the sensation of being withdrawn and isolated, it is always participating in the vital processes that fill the thoroughfares and byways of the psyche to which it belongs. Spirit is not an idle observer. Like everything else in nature, it has a job to do. It is the control center for values that the organism imagines and creates through the fabrication of ideals and the selective pursuit of them. Spirit is the locus and domain of enjoyment as a gratifying possibility for consciousness and the mind. The fulfillment of appetitive behavior need not include any awareness of itself. In most of psyche, for instance in the vegetative part that constitutes so much of our being, it does not. But when fulfillment of any sort takes center stage, when it presents itself as consummatory experience self-consciously desired by an organism, it forms the particular segment within psyche which is spirit.

Santayana separates spirit and psyche; I suggest that they can be properly understood only by seeing that they are unified, spirit being a subdivision within psyche and imbued with the same material reality. There is no independent realm of spirit. Though spirit may think it is detached, it is still part of the mainland. Spirit will often fail to modify nature as it would like, but its sense of being cast out— which varies greatly and cannot be total—is itself a vital response rather than being proof of causal inefficacy. And though suffering is the lot of the perceptive spirit living in a brutish world that would seem to have no final interest in the goods that spirit craves and also creates, there is no justification for defining spirit in terms of its potentiality for suffering. Spirit can be profoundly joyful, and is so whenever it fully realizes its success in pursuing values that matter to it and will survive for a period of time. When that happens, the nature in us feels itself at home in nature at large. Spirit is in fact nature transcending itself from within, which is the only kind of transcendence it allows.

If we accept this line of reasoning, we may reach a clearer vision of how human beings can have a valid faith in nature. Schopenhauer excludes this possibility because he is so extreme in his conception of existence as bloodied o'er by its own random hideousness. Santayana talks, more judiciously, of "animal faith," but he uses that idea to explain the irrational impulse that enables even an epistemological skeptic to go on living in the world about which, theoretically, he can never have any knowledge. Neither Santayana nor Schopenhauer appreciates the faith that pantheism makes central in its adoration of nature. Without being an advocate of pantheism, I see how its reverential attitude can possibly overcome the doubts and disabilities inherent in the philosophies of both Schopenhauer and Santayana.

At the same time, I recognize how much these philosophers help us to understand the problems that every enlightened spirit must confront. The proud defiance of nature that Schopenhauer proclaims will not enable us to escape our tragic fate, as he admits, but it does illuminate a possible dignity that Schopenhauer bravely enunciates. Similarly, Santayana's ideas about spirit's awareness of a universal good that may always conflict with the good for any individual, including the person to whom spirit itself belongs, vividly portray the moral difficulties all human beings face at every moment. Moreover, Santayana's further notion that spirit seeks to love the love in everything is infinitely suggestive and worthy of continued exploration.

Schopenhauer and Santayana, each in his own way, reflect the failure of nerve that spread throughout the world during the century between their death dates. They are masterful representatives of that crisis in post-Romantic thought, as well as being great artists depicting in their philosophical genre the truth about themselves and their own particular condition as human beings. I have no desire to denigrate the work of these major thinkers. I have criticized them in the hope of resolving some of the dilemmas they pose. We may thereby gain a more thorough understanding of how aesthetics is foundational to ethics as well as religion. The naturalistic conception of art, ethics, and religion that will ensue may possibly be more satisfying than theirs.

Ethical and religious attitudes interweave not only with the biological processes they are designed to orient but also with each other. In the introduction to this book, I spoke of artists as if they can sometimes be secular saints. I could have said the same about devoted men and women of action. But though this way of thinking may be useful as an indication of how spirituality has pertinence for everyday life, it raises problems of its own. In general, saints are rightly thought to be different from heroes; the saintly disposition might even seem inimical to the heroic. But though the two conditions have often been directed toward alternate goals, one toward heaven and the other toward Valhalla or some earthly paradise, they consist of similar elements organized in configurations that are not the same.

Saints, or saintly persons, are people who efface and sometimes sacrifice themselves in the name of some all-embracing belief. They display a sense of relative worthlessness in contrast to whatever their faith holds aloft as supremely good. Christian martyrs are not considered to be saints *simply* because they choose death rather than betrayal of their religion. It is something else, their demonstration of submissiveness or self-renunciation, that causes the acts culminating in martyrdom to be deemed saintly. Though saints are often tormented by awareness of what they call their sinful state, they become serene, even happy, as they approximate and approach the final extinction of their natural cravings. Death is welcomed as a fulfillment, since it completes the desired project of self-elimination through faith alone.

The heroic attitude would seem to be totally different from that. We think of the hero standing erect on ramparts that symbolize a noble cause, his chest swelling with aggressive enthusiasm as he defies all opposition to his self-assertiveness. Though he is ready to impose his will upon fallible humanity or recalcitrant nature, he acts to destroy evil and to promote the greatest good of those who need his strength of purpose. He can carry out his mission, however, only if he resembles the saint in being willing to sacrifice himself. He may not court self-destruction as the saintly martyr does, but he will run the risk of death whenever it is required by the ends he serves.

At this point the phenomenologies of saint and hero begin to converge. The hero pursues some elevated achievement, awe inspiring to the rest of us and beyond our intellectual or emotional ability to devote ourselves to this goal (assuming we even recognize its ideality). But though the hero struggles with fate instead of submitting as others do, he resembles the saint in giving himself to the possible value toward which his efforts are directed. The hero must always content himself with having led his people to some promised land that he will never enter. If he acts for self-aggrandizement, he is not a real hero. On the other hand, a person who truly is a saint must renounce himself for motives other than a love of death or self-punishment. He must be selfless and willing to die, but only for the sake of ideals he considers affirmative and of primary importance in some ultimate sense, whether or not they are transcendental.

In this area of overlap, we discern the spirituality of both the saintly and the heroic attitude. Mere readiness for death is not a proof of spiritual devotion. Any pitiful suicide or mercenary soldier going into battle may be prepared to die. What distinguishes both the saint and the hero is the fact that they have before them something that *justifies* their death, something that compels them to subordinate all else in life to its inherent goodness. The saint says no to himself but yes to the grandeur he ascribes to divinity; the hero says yes to whatever life-augmenting force he molds to serve humanity and other creatures but no to anything in himself that would deflect him from his ideal. For both saint and hero alike, dying is but an incidental occurrence, appropriate as a demonstration of faith but not itself a rationale for what they do.

In a further dimension, saint and hero are "absolute for death." That phrase occurs in Shakespeare's *Measure for Measure*.[2] Visiting Claudio in prison, the duke has disguised himself as a friar, and as such he tries to help the condemned man face up to his imminent execution. We intuit that the duke will not let Claudio die. And in fact he wants him to live, provided he can learn the great lesson of existence, which is that if we accept the necessity of death as a precondition for life we thus acquire the ability to endure all hardships with equanimity. Whether Claudio dies that day or many years in the future, it is absolute that sooner if not later, and for one reason or another, he *will* die. Knowing this, feeling it deeply within himself in everything he does, Claudio will have reached a level of spirituality that the duke impersonates in dressing as a friar. Saints and heroes are people, different among themselves in many other ways, who have mastered this message and developed the fortitude to construct a spiritual life coherent with it.

In order to live ethically, one does not have to be a hero, as one also does not have to be a saint in order to be religious. Heroism and saintliness are therefore equally anomalous. The hero strives for a perfection of rectitude that defines some code of right and wrong. To be ethical, however, one need only live up to that code in the sense that one acts, as a matter of duty, not to violate it. But no one, not even the hero, is obligated to have the perfectionist commitment that makes people into heroes. Heroism is supererogatory, incapable of being required of anyone. We often feel guilty if we transgress in relation to the code we accept, but only rarely if we fail to be heroes. While those who do their duty are thought to be commendable, those who strive for heroism are revered as exemplars of whatever ethical idealism they represent.

Why should this be the case? It is often harder to do the dutiful thing despite one's inclination to be selfish than it is—for the hero, at least—to throw oneself into the passions of heroic action. The hero is rewarded by his sheer ability to act freely, and with total dedication; he is doing what he fervently believes in. Perhaps we should save our reverence for the plodding, and usually unrecognized, servant of the Lord who quietly adheres to conscience and to duty.

The situation is similar with respect to saintliness. There, too, we may wonder whether it is a greater sign of spirituality to give one's life, quite literally, as the martyrs do, than to keep the faith in the daily but routine manner of a devout believer. I raise this issue not in the hope of finding a solution but rather to illustrate how questions about living the ethical or religious life may be irresolvable. In most of its operations, nature forces us to make a definite though somewhat variable response. When boulders are falling, we cannot equivocate; we must get out of the way if we want to survive, though where we leap will depend on personal judgment. But in giving life to spirit, nature permits an indeterminacy that prevents us from ever being sure that the values we create have any superiority over others, or even authenticity in terms of what we ourselves are and wish to be.

❄

For this reason, philosophers may never reach agreement about the normative goals of ethical theory. The Kantian school will structure its analysis on the basis of some ideal rationality that determines what is right or wrong universally; the utilitarians will argue that only general happiness, whatever it may be, can serve as the standard of good or bad and therefore right or wrong; the intuitionists will claim that all such matters depend on direct inspection of one's conscience, even if that is just a product of society and the local environment. But all these governing criteria, important as they are for those who bestow value on them, are equally arbitrary in the sense that nothing can possibly prove the necessity of adhering to one rather than the other. They are equal as aesthetic artifacts of the moral and idealizing imagination. They are creative expressions of the human spirit, original or innovative just like works of fine art. If we argue for or against them, or competing standards, we do so as artists do when they offer their own perspective on the world presented through some new approach to meaning and technique.

In the issues that religious thinkers have usually addressed, there is a comparable indeterminacy and consequent dependence on individual imagination. Traditional religions, particularly in the West, have often maintained that human beings possess an immortal soul, and that after death they will become acquainted with a different order of being, called "eternity," which explains the life in nature we now experience while also being a transcendence of it. The idea that we can possibly live for an indefinite duration, perhaps forever, is difficult to understand but not incomprehensible. To make sense of it, we would have to hypothesize about technologies in medicine or space travel. But these developments, fictional as they might seem, would still be explicable as potentialities in nature and our progressive manipulation of it. That is not the immortality with which religious thinkers usually concern themselves. They believe in an existence without termination that the soul will have once it has been liberated from the body. And by soul, they mean something related to, though in principle quite different from, mind or consciousness as these appear in the order of temporality. How can we decide whether their notion is or is not true, or even worth considering?

I do not think we can. It would not do, for instance, to argue that all the billions of human beings who have lived thus far, plus those who are still unborn, could not be supported for an endless period in the universe as we know it. That argument was posed to me by a scientist who attended a public lecture I gave on the meaning of death. But obviously the religious theorists are asking us to envisage a realm of being that is not knowable to us in our present universe, or in our dispensation as natural entities. What, then, are we talking about? No answer can be given without invoking metaphoric possibilities that imagination calls forth in this kind of discourse but cannot comprehend except as a daydream—which is to say, as a work of art that has no necessary correspondence with any factual condition.

This kind of difficulty recurs in relevant questions about our mortality. Some philosophers have thought that death is always an evil, regardless of the age at which one dies or the contents of the experience that is destroyed by our extinction. In *The Creation of Value* I argued that death is an evil only if the life it cuts short is worth living. Although I tried throughout that book, and elsewhere, to discover what it is that makes life valuable, I offered no explicit decision procedure for determining whether death is or is not an evil in any particular case. Moreover, there may be persons, terminal patients for instance, whose condition seems hopelessly unredeemable but who nevertheless have access to goods of which we cannot know. To that extent, the issue of whether death must always be an evil may well be irresolvable in principle.

All moral and religious queries about death pose a similar problem. At every stage of life there are elements of experience that baffle us and may defy comprehension, even by those who benefit from them. How can we know, for instance, whether the death of an infant is or is not more tragic than the death of an older person? We are generally inclined to believe this, though some religious people sound as if they think the infant's death is not at all tragic since the greater innocence of its soul gives it a better chance of going to heaven. But most of us would say that in itself the death of a very young boy or girl is more terrible than the death of someone who has lived a long time. From the point of view of species survival, that belief is certainly appropriate insofar as the old are less capable of reproductive behavior than the young. On the other hand, they may know more about the living of a good life, they are often less harmful to others, and they sometimes—depending on the individual—have cultivated through the years uniquely precious talents. If a doctor with a miraculous cure for rheumatic fever had to choose between saving either Mozart at age thirty-five or a drug-infected neonate, there being no way of saving both, is it not likely that he would feel justified in letting the neonate die?

One might argue that a lottery or other random choice should settle such matters, since the baby has a right to live equal to Mozart's. But that right is not automatic or conclusive in every case. If the neonate was totally demented and doomed to suffer greatly throughout its life, we might well agree that it should not be given priority over Mozart. In a situation such as this one, we may feel confident about our choice of who shall live and who shall die. We may likewise believe that, in view of the horrible existence the child would have, this particular death is not an evil. But we have no way of telling *how much* the bad components in experience must outweigh the good ones in order for us to say that death is or is not an evil under all circumstances in general.

From this, it follows that even when we can make rational and justifiable decisions—Mozart and not the unfortunate neonate shall live—we do so without a great deal of knowledge about the meaning or ontology of death. Since that is what I also concluded about immortality, I am led to wonder whether any religious doctrines in these matters can be worthy of belief. Even in issues related to the nature of life, there lingers a kind of indeterminacy that stymies our longings for metaphysical truths. I know by acquaintance what life and consciousness are in myself, but can I know what they are in others?

We assume that other people have experiences comparable to our own, and out of that assumption we construct linguistic and diversely symbolic means of communication and interpretation. When all goes well, we believe that we make contact with someone's inner state. It is as if we have found a window into the habitation of a separate consciousness. When things go extremely well, as they do for intuitive and highly perceptive people, we may feel assured that understanding of another person's life has been acquired. But even at its best, acquaintance with someone else's being must always remain partial and schematic. The *feeling* of what it is to be alive, the sense of past and present with all the infinitely complex responses that throb through them, the accretion of meanings that constitute a unique and autonomous identity—little of this can be transferred from one person to another with any certainty, however strong the mutual attunement between these persons.

If this is true of members of the same human species, how imperfect must our comprehension of other creatures be! Even if we treat our dogs and cats as fellow participants in life with whom we can communicate despite the differences in our intellects, we have hardly any idea of what they really experience. We know they get hungry since they seek for food; we know from their actual choices that they prefer one kind of food rather than another; we know when they are replete, for then their searching and ingestion come to an end. If they sit in the sun and do nothing, we assume they are savoring the sweetness of mere existence, mindlessly enjoying these moments of unperturbed quiescence. They may also display some hunting, playful, and reproductive behavior; and we observe that, like other animals, they have intricate patterns of sociability that they extend to us as well. But what is their consciousness like? We realize they are different from us in many respects, but just how different we can never know. They do not have the conceptual equipment that we have, and clearly they do not fear death or ponder over the meaning of everything as we do. Despite our frequent tendency to humanize other animals, and regardless of our ability to love them and to be loved by them, their minds and general apperception of reality are largely incomprehensible to us.

I mention these puzzling questions about life because they represent the mysteries that confront us in the cosmos pervasively and because they reinforce my belief that religion as well as ethics is founded on aesthetics. There are two ways in which we might cope with these universal mysteries: we could take them as a kind of Pandora's box, best left unexamined, or else we could respond by creating meaningful accounts of everything from our own point of view. With its ranging faculties of imagination and idealization, humankind has usually chosen the latter path. It makes the mysterious intelligible, even though there is no rational authority for extrapolating beyond our own experience.

In pursuing this direction, the imaginative process is very beguiling. When our species lived in close rapport with physical nature, imagination constructed anthropomorphic religions. Although idealized with respect to power, cunning, or even goodness, the gods were seen as projections of what is familiar to us as human beings and therefore not entirely mysterious. When our mode of life began to change as a result of achievements in technology and science, each relying on innovations that creatively exceed our concrete existence, imagination fabricated ethereal notions of deities who exist apart from nature, make everything out of nothing, defy the laws of either logic or common sense, and even thrive outside time and space. The newer religions were also anthropomorphic to some degree, for imagination cannot operate in a vacuum, and they appeared as an idealization of science. They sought to provide knowledge about the entire universe without having to resort to empirical methods of verification. Our imagination has never flourished more extravagantly.

In the modern era many philosophers have grappled with the relationship between religion and the sciences. In the next chapter I will return to my suggestion that the play of imagination, which is also a serious enterprise, explains their dependence on each other.

Here I want to suggest that even highly sophisticated thinkers like William James are often mistaken in their approach to this issue. James was aware that knowledge of the world must normally come from scientific, or at least quasi-scientific, procedures. But religion presents itself as superscience based on faith, and therefore it does not justify its dogmas by reference to the evidence that empirical knowledge requires. James refused to repudiate religion on those grounds, however, and neither did he think that scruples about rationality should force us to suspend judgment. He defended the idea of a "will to believe" in circumstances in which the evidence is balanced, or inconclusive, and therefore inadequate for making a purely rational decision. James thought that under those conditions we are free to believe as we wish. Although the conflicting views are equally unsubstantiated, James maintained, we need not withhold belief, since a choice of one or the other alternative will lead to different practical consequences, and that can justify our having faith (or else refusing to).

James's reasoning is persuasive in part but also weakened by the fact that a justification in terms of consequences is not the same as a justification in terms of evidence, and in religious questions there are no objective criteria for choosing between these modes of justification. If the evidence for or against some possibility is perfectly balanced, we may properly believe in accordance with our preferences among the consequences. But this does not preclude our suspending judgment if we decide to believe only what is based on sufficient evidence. That is always an option for those who wish to extend the methodology of science to religious debates and thus use it as the arbiter of belief. Remaining faithful to the data of experience, reaching no conclusions they do not warrant, cannot be the *only* method for dealing legitimately with issues in religion or metaphysics. But it is never an inappropriate way to handle such problems, even if they have important consequences.

James tried to support his position by arguing that, for all practical purposes, suspending judgment about religion is tantamount to accepting a negative point of view. If one cannot decide whether the statement "God exists" is true or false, one forfeits the comfort

and assurance made possible by faith in God's existence, and therefore to that extent there is practically, in terms of consequences, no
difference between denying the existence of God and suspending
judgment about it. I think James is right, but only if one limits the
relevant consequences to the kind that he specifies. In doing so,
however, he neglects other consequences, those that come from
withholding judgment because of supervening scruples about believing beyond the evidence. These consequences are very different
from the ones that follow upon the accepting or rejecting of traditional dogmas. A person who chooses to suspend judgment and
remain agnostic, or for all institutional purposes nonbelieving, has
decided to live a life that is not the same as being either a devotee or
an opponent of some theistic faith. He finds and creates meaning in
life where these others do not. Cultivating fidelity to observable
facts, he cherishes standards of intellectual rectitude that are quite
different from theirs.

I offer this critique of James's thinking about the will to believe
in order to emphasize the role of imagination and idealization in all
such matters. By defending the will to believe as he does, James
manifests an idealistic attitude whose value other philosophers may
be willing to discard. In his tenderhearted way, James wants to make
available to suffering humanity the emotional benefits that religion
can yield even when it has no scientific credibility. Those who con-
demn him for encouraging what they call a will to make-believe are
responding to the appeal of another ideal—adherence to truths
established by a preponderance of empirical evidence. Religious
devotees may readily agree that this criterion is the right one in
science or ordinary common sense, but they claim that it is not
relevant to the search for metaphysical and theological certitude.
With that as their meaning in life, they harken to different ideals
and exercise a different type of imagination.

I recognize no authority, whether in reason or feeling or elsewhere in our nature, that can justifiably tell us how to choose
between attitudes such as these. They are all, equally, products of
the human ability to entertain and employ anything that can help us
get through life. The entertaining and the employing are created

freely, not in the sense that nothing causes them but only because nothing in the objective circumstances requires them to be the same for different individuals. They exemplify what I call the bestowal of value, which is an aesthetic phenomenon and an agency of spirit.

Though we tend to identify the spiritual life with religious attitudes, I want to emphasize that ethical dispositions are no less representative of spirituality. As formulated through conceptions of good and bad, right and wrong, an ethical code is an expression of imagination, together with idealization, determining what is permissible in relations among people or between the human race and other species. All philosophical systems are alike in creating general though often detailed presentations of whatever ideals enliven the imagination of some originator.

Since these systems are inevitably abstract, however, they can stretch imagination to a point where its utility becomes, paradoxically, diminished. I may have imagination enough to understand the meaning of the categorical imperative, or of the standard of the greatest good of the greatest number, or of goodness as a quality that human beings intuit, and yet find myself incapable of solving many of the practical and moral issues that arise throughout my life. Each ethical system can be dismissed as summarily as Mill does with Kant's in a paragraph of *Utilitarianism*, and as Nietzsche does with Mill's, and as Santayana with G. E. Moore's. But also the different theories can be applied in such variable ways that imagination may quickly founder in a sea of ambiguity. Though technical philosophers exercise their own imaginative talents by dealing with the technicalities of this situation, they diverge among themselves, and most other people feel constrained to use different modes of reasoning in order to handle their ethical problems.

Searching for an alternate, possibly better, type of imagination, naturalistic relativists such as Dewey and Santayana say "act with intelligence," or "know thyself." These are edifying suggestions, but they do not help very much, and when Dewey and Santayana spell out the implications of their ethical beliefs, they, too, revert to abstract presuppositions that imagination embroiders with as little substantiation as in the more tendentious systems of morality. In all alike, the painful complexities of human existence remain at least partly unresolved. It is not enough to articulate decision procedures that tell people what to do in representative situations, or how to regulate uncontrolled behavior, as in children or criminals. We also need to cope with the specific feelings and inclinations that exist at every moment of our active life. No ethical system can generate that capacity from within itself. At this point the philosophical imagination must recognize its own limitations.

As if to compensate for this inadequacy, imagination probes to a less cognitive but more affective level of our being, one that it alone has access to. A guide to this particular mode of operation can be found in an essay that Percy Bysshe Shelley wrote in defense of poetry. Praising that art form because it shows imagination functioning as an ethical force, Shelley describes imagination's ability to create what he calls "sympathetic identification" with other people. Shelley portrays that as the basis of all true morality: "A man, to be greatly good, must imagine intensely and comprehensively; he must put himself in the place of another and of many others; the pains and pleasures of his species must become his own. The great instrument of the moral good is the imagination."[3]

This capacity to put oneself in another's position is an aptitude that is requisite whatever one's system of ethics may be. The imaginative idealizations that construct the governing standards in Kantian, utilitarian, intuitionist, or other philosophy are insufficient for the application of these standards to actual situations. Lived experience is fraught with infinitely numerous idiosyncrasies that exist in every circumstance that demands some decision on our part. We can act judiciously, and in harmony with the principles of our ethical code, only by an additional act of sympathetic imagination that puts us in touch with particular feelings and interests that motivate others as well as oneself. We may be able to inspect our own inclinations directly, but to appreciate what anyone else needs and wants and considers indispensable for a good life requires imaginative responses of this special sort.

Like all attempts to understand another bit of life from its own point of view, this type of imagination is highly fallible and uncertain. Some people, those we admire for their convincing and rapidly formed perceptions, seem almost godlike in their relative success in this area. Most of us are backward in varying degrees and therefore must follow general rules that articulate and condense what the moral geniuses have conveyed as the fruit of their experience in the world. But even they have only limited insight, and no ultimate authority.

Since life is so greatly disparate, and since individual occasions of it—in nonhuman as well as human beings—are unique entities within themselves, our ability to imagine another's condition is hardly predictable in its outcome. Nor can this art be taught in any rigorous manner, though its achievements may be emulated and developed. Once we emancipate affective imagination from the wilder presuppositions that Shelley and other Romantics inherited from their religious origins, we may see it as an aesthetic, albeit spiritual, basis of morality as well as religion. Even the relativist, or one who accepts a modified version of different ethical systems, may feel the need to further this aspect of human nature. The question still remaining, however, is whether the project can ever succeed.

In the following chapter, I suggest some reasons for thinking that the concept of sympathetic identification is not adequate for understanding our ability to respond to another person's identity. Nevertheless, that concept will encourage us to explore the ways in which empathy, sympathy, and compassion are simultaneously both ethical and religious phenomena. Being an overlap between social and religious love, they indicate a gamut of feelings, developmental within our nature, that can be spiritual as well as natural. If only to that extent, religion is based upon the same kind of imagination as morality.

Approaching ethics and religion in this fashion, we see that they cannot be separated by the bifurcation imposed by earlier philosophers or theologians. Ethical responses are an expression of what is native to our being, and also a manifestation of spiritual attainment. In its own way, morality is the harmonization of psyche and spirit.

It is spirit not in isolation from matter but rather interacting as an imaginative, and sometimes beautiful, reconstitution of material necessities that it transforms into an expressive and highly meaningful pattern of life. Ethics then merges with aesthetics, spirit realizes its locus, its suitable function in nature, and the world is enriched by the fact that at least some of its inhabitants are able to perfect the art of living. As in all art, meaning and happiness are thereby integrated. The resulting consummations make life worth living to that degree.

❋

For its part, religion, too, will have a different configuration once we overcome the idea that it must be alien to the natural order. Saintly devotion to the welfare of others is a form of life that does not have to justify itself in terms of any supernatural edict. It is part of our humanity, and those who have the requisite will and fortitude reveal that ethics and religion can join forces in a common effort even if their primordial idealizations are not the same.

In reaching for the soul of another, the religious saint employs the same affective imagination that enables the heroic atheist to alleviate suffering in those he wants to help. Moreover, religion builds its ideological edifice out of the bricks and mortar of naturalistic myths and legends that imagination also proffers. This much of religion is literature at its most philosophical. Religion is not just a projection of wish fulfillments, as Freud thought, or even an allegorization of them. While emanating from needs and desires that human beings experience as creatures of nature, it can help its adherents to grapple with the mysteries that continually surround us in life. The conceptualization that is present in all religions is an imaginative, though sometimes ridiculous, mixture of science, storytelling, moralizing, social instruction, and individual or group self-affirmation.

That is why the religious life is so prevalent in human experience. Endowed with the remarkable forces of imagination and idealization that belong to our species as it has evolved, we have a strong impulse to wonder and to speculate about everything in life, to dramatize possible solutions for fundamental questions about the universe, and to formulate explanations that make our moment-by-moment existence more rewarding and more meaningful. If our use of imagination and idealization remains faithful to the realities of our nature, and of nature in general, the spirituality created in this process can never degenerate into negativity. Its goodness is humane as well as devotional, while also being moral and aesthetic.

Religious art and music effect this unity in a context of emotional benefit for those who gather to reenact their chosen faith. But even nonbelievers can share in these precious artifacts. They need only recognize that in the sounds they hear, or the fables they see and read, human inventiveness has created a harmony between nature and that much of itself which is spirit. The value of that is obvious, and for many people quite sufficient for the good life.

LOVE, MEANING,
HAPPINESS

❧

Since I have argued that ethics and religion, and the life of spirit as a whole, have their foundation in the aesthetic aspect of our experience, some critics will complain that my view recognizes no objectivity in any of the values that human beings have cherished and even revered. It may also be suggested that philosophy such as mine divests ethics, religion, and possibly aesthetics itself of any specifiable content. If this were true, one might infer that my conception of nature as well as spirit, to say nothing of their harmonization, is not only untenable but also devoid of any relevance to the problems of men and women in the real world.

To preclude charges such as these, one must explicate—in greater detail than I have done thus far—the place in nature that defines the spirituality of whatever values belong to ethics, religion, and art. The linchpin of my argument can be found in the concepts of empathy, sympathy, and compassion that are analyzed briefly in *The Pursuit of Love*. Amplifying that discussion, we do well to begin with Schopenhauer's writings on the foundation of morals. Schopenhauer faced a problem in his philosophy similar to mine, and his solution may help us to proceed.

In *The Basis of Morality* Schopenhauer rejects attempts to provide a metaphysical grounding for ethical behavior that have traditionally been made by rationalists in philosophy and by apologists for

Western religion. As against Kant, for instance, Schopenhauer looks for something in human nature that is deeper than reason and can better sustain our ideas about good and bad, right and wrong, virtue and vice. He asserts that in itself a selfish concern about one's own welfare is never bad, wrong, or vicious. Nature operates through the self-orienting interests that motivate everything that lives. If a person hunts down and kills an animal in order to eat it, this alone is not ethically relevant—it is neither right nor wrong—since the harm done to the unfortunate prey has been caused by a normal and natural selfish need. If, however, someone injures another creature unnecessarily, wantonly or for sport, such conduct serves no selfish end and is therefore evil. It is an unjustifiable act of malice. According to Schopenhauer, ethics consists in specifying the principles that enable us to live selfishly and to our own advantage without engaging in malicious behavior.

There are two ethical principles that Schopenhauer considers basic in human nature. One is justice; the other is nonsexual love, what the translators call "loving-kindness." The former is negative: it ordains the conditions under which one shall not bring harm to another living entity. The latter is positive: it issues from an affective impetus in our being that makes us *want* to help other people, and even forms of life quite different from our own. The attitude that embodies this positive concern is *Mitleid*, usually translated as "compassion," though when Schopenhauer approvingly quotes from Rousseau, he seems willing to accept the French word *pitié* ("pity").

Through compassion, as Schopenhauer interprets it, a person identifies himself with some other creature. This act of identification provides the sanction that justice needs, since it overrides whatever tendency to malice may arise in ordinary experience. When identification shows itself as loving-kindness toward a person or animal whose welfare one tries to increase, it directly reveals the compassionate element of human nature. Compassion is a response to the presence of suffering in the other being. It is not definable as any pleasure or happiness that life may encompass. Since Schopenhauer believes that happiness is only secondary, a minor element in nature, he considers compassion toward the pain, the sorrow, the mental and physical suffering of all life as morally more profound than any delight that we may feel because another has garnered some good fortune. Only through compassion do we react with understanding to the universal tragedy inherent in animate existence.

Schopenhauer repeatedly asserts that the mere occurrence of compassion, as well as the sense of identification that manifests it in action, is mysterious and possibly incomprehensible. To account for its appearance in nature, he offers a metaphysical explanation. He says that through Mitleid we penetrate to the deepest truth about our reality. In the selfishness of daily existence we think that we are, each of us, individuals whose special personality issues from our uniqueness and irreplaceable autonomy. According to Schopenhauer, this is an illusion created by the intellect as part of its pragmatic attempt to preserve life. In reality there are no individuals: life is a single totality to which we all belong as expressions of its fluid oneness rather than as separate entities. Compassion is the positive and honest recognition of this fact. Through it we perceive that what we are is indistinguishable from what other human or nonhuman creatures are. We are all not only fellow sufferers in the monstrosity of existence but also *identical*, inasmuch as we share the same ultimate condition. We are merely aspects of the unitary will, the vital force of nature, which courses through us and ineluctably fuses us with one another. As a statement of this metaphysical creed in which he believes, Schopenhauer remarks:

> "Individuation is merely an appearance. . . . Hence also the plurality and difference of individuals is but a phenomenon, that is, exist only in my mental picture. My true innermost being subsists in every living thing, just really, as directly in my own consciousness it is evidenced only to myself." This is the higher knowledge: for which there is in Sanskrit the standing formula, *tat tvam asi*, "that art thou." Out of the depths of human nature it wells up in the shape of Compassion, and is therefore the source of all genuine, that is, disinterested virtue.[1]

Schopenhauer's reference to the Hindu concept of universal fusion as fundamental in being as a whole alerts us to a recurrent difficulty in his metaphysics. As I have argued in various places, fusion or merging is a physical, often chemical, event that does occur, but not as a characteristic of life in animals. Human beings in particular do not merge with one another, even when they are unified through the molten fervor of sexual passion. Some men and women idealize merging and make it the principal goal of their existence; the meaning in their lives results from their longing for a fusion with an actual or imagined person. But the kind of unity they seek, often under the influence of a Romantic ideology whose origin in Western culture is fairly recent, runs counter to our human nature. However intimate their relationship, people cannot lose their separate identity. However ardent or loving their oneness may be, they always remain unique and autonomous individuals. Their love may unite them, as their mutual hatred would if it was sufficiently intense, but neither the greatest love nor the greatest hatred can alter the indefeasibility of their being different persons. Merging of the sort that Schopenhauer alludes to must therefore be impossible.

✳

In saying this, I am hewing closer to empirical data than Schopenhauer does. But can I claim to be any less metaphysical in my judgments? As much as I would like to say yes, I must admit that my repudiation of merging as an ultimate state of being in human life is just as nonverifiable as his assertion of it. Each of us is extrapolating beyond our ordinary experience in ways that our contrasting imagination diversely employs to create incompatible idealizations of the world. One might say that, in an issue such as this, we differ in our sense of reality. I am willing to leave it there. And though Schopenhauer often sounds like a dogmatist when he articulates his metaphysics, he may well have agreed that at this level of our reasoning we both rely on leaps of imagination just as artists do when they present visions of the world that are vastly different from one another.

What makes Schopenhauer's vision particularly valuable and supportive for my thinking is the fact that he considers compassion, whatever its metaphysical meaning, as the basis of morality. That seems to me an infinitely fruitful and suggestive idea. It frees us from Kantian-type rationalism, which is, as Schopenhauer states, foreign to what most people feel in ethical situations; and it helps to clarify what Hume, Rousseau, and Mill were groping for in their emphasis upon the primacy of humanitarian sentiment. Moreover, in his great concern about the suffering of all living things, Schopenhauer correctly insists that each of them is worthy of the same compassionate feelings that human beings would receive in a moral order.

At the same time, I believe, Schopenhauer's conception needs revision and further development. *Mitleid* literally means "suffering with." But that is ambiguous, as indicated by the fact that the English translators sometimes render the German word as "sympathy" and sometimes as "compassion," even though these have different connotations. The term *pitié* that Schopenhauer borrows from Rousseau adds to the confusion and probably should be avoided straightaway. Pity implies an attitude of condescension that is unlike the response Schopenhauer has in mind.

We feel pity toward those with whom we do *not* identify ourselves. Pity can make us sad that someone is suffering, but it need not involve any further feeling or behavior on our part. We may or may not take another's suffering upon ourselves, either by undergoing something comparable as in sympathy or by performing actions that are compassionate inasmuch as they attempt to relieve his or her distress. In experiencing pity, we remain aware of our *difference* from the other person: for we are glad that it is not we who are suffering, even if we regret that anyone else should be. Our condescension consists in the separation between these sentiments. This disposition is not venal or unethical, which might be the case if we gloried at another's misfortune or observed it with disdain. All the same, and well intentioned as we may be, pity can scarcely serve as the basis of morality.

One might say that only sympathy is needed, as argued by the eighteenth- and nineteenth-century adherents to the doctrine of "sympathetic identification" mentioned earlier. But the inadequacies of that conception are indicated from the outset by the fact that the terminology is, so to speak, overly determined. It refers to identification that is also a mode of sympathy, which is, however, a vastly different kind of response. In *The Pursuit of Love* I distinguished between sympathy and empathy as a prelude to a more thorough account of the discrepancy between these affective modes. In the present context I can resume the analysis by citing a bit of Gilbert and Sullivan. Toward the beginning of *Trial by Jury*, the defendant in a breach-of-promise suit tells the jury how he fell in love with the girl who has now brought him to court, how he professed his love effusively but in time found the young lady to be a "bore intense," and how, one morning, he became another's lovesick boy. This recital is given in an effort to arouse the sympathy of the (all-male) jury. But it fails in that attempt, not because the jurors cannot empathize with the defendant but because they do so. They sing:

> Oh, I was like that when a lad!
>   A shocking young scamp of a rover,
> I behaved like a regular cad;
>   But that sort of thing is all over.
> I'm now a respectable chap
>   And shine with a virtue resplendent
> And, therefore, I haven't a scrap
>   Of sympathy with the defendant!

We laugh at this comic switch of expectations because we suddenly realize that the association between sympathy and empathetic identification to which we have become accustomed is erroneous. The two can go together, but not inevitably, and when their simultaneous occurrence becomes a virtue, that results from an experience of sympathy which is different from mere identification. For this reason alone, our ability to identify with another person does not lend itself to the kind of explanation that Schopenhauer suggests. As in the jury's song, identification signifies an empathetic response that puts us in the other's position in the sense that we recognize how we are alike, similar in behavior as well as feeling, but not as a matter of sympathy or any merged oneness. Empathy may be a frequent concomitant of sympathy, and possibly a necessary condition for it to occur, but the idea of fusion is irrelevant to both.

Through empathy we can perceive our kinship with another, and even show it, as in the classic example of spectators leaning forward as they watch runners at the starting line who are crouched in anticipation of the initiating pistol shot. To a minimal degree this manifests a bestowal of value, since the spectators have given so much importance to the physical and mental condition of the runners that they, too, are straining to launch their bodies. But since there is no suggestion of benevolence or good will in this empathetic gesture, it would be hard to imagine that it reveals the nature of either loving-kindness or morality.

For these to exist, we must undergo feelings of sympathy that put us in the other's position through a process of affective imagination. In having sympathy for the other creature, we sense what it must be feeling and we care about that in a way that is comparable to our caring about our own experience. Although we know that we and the object of our attention are not identical, we identify *with* it as a manifestation of our concern *for* it. That represents a significant bestowal of value and warrants considering our response a demonstration of love.

Yet even sympathy cannot support morality as a whole. For one thing, sympathy implies feelings in detachment from their material expression. The consummatory condition that many Romantics envisaged was a sympathetic bond that joined the souls or minds or disembodied consciousness of elective affinities. Though the language was often metaphoric and could not be taken otherwise, it suggested an incorporeal unity that earth in all its earthiness does not afford. To this extent, the Romantic idea ignored sympathy's great reliance upon the attunement between the bodies of different creatures. Yet that is essential if they are to communicate their loving attitude. Sympathetic response need not be confined to consciousness or a meeting of minds. It may also be directed toward the physical.

With their lessened intellect and self-awareness, nonhuman animals must experience this aspect of sympathy more consistently than we do. A cat's maternal love exhibits her spontaneous concern about her kitten's material well-being but shows no interest in a felt oneness with its consciousness. Both animals will enjoy their physical contact, as human beings also do with one another or with other animals, but this symphysis between their bodies is different from the sympathy that most philosophers have idealized.[2]

On the other hand, as I argued in *The Pursuit of Love*, sympathy can often be nothing but a feeling. It may never issue into action that benefits whatever creature happens to elicit it. Our sympathetic feeling can establish an affective, even emotional bond, but without our ever doing anything to alleviate the suffering to which we are responding. In that event our sympathetic identification is not definitive of either ethics or religion. At its best, it serves as an instigating motive that awakens us to the need for action; at its worst, it is a palliative that comforts us by creating a feckless sense of oneness.

Sympathy becomes the basis of morality or truly spiritual love only when its latency for intervention becomes kinetic, when the feeling of identification shows itself in conduct that effectively changes the world, when we immerse ourselves through action to modify the condition of the person or animal who is suffering, when we take that suffering upon ourselves. If this occurs, our sympathy has been transformed into something else. It has become a part of what can authentically be called compassion.

The confusion between sympathy and compassion may possibly result from etymology of the latter term. Broken into its Latin components, it seems to mean a state of suffering-with. The same is true of Mitleid. But compassion, as distinct from sympathy, requires more than just the fact that two or more individuals are being united by a single or similar suffering. In acting for the welfare of the one who suffers, the compassionate person makes that suffering his own but does not duplicate it. He does not perpetuate the other's feelings, which may be painful and therefore piteous, but rather he attends to them as unwelcome ingredients in circumstances that must be altered. Through compassion we are with the other person as agents in a humanitarian enterprise and not merely as affective resonators. Though we may have no desire to sacrifice ourselves, we involve our entire being in another's predicament by orienting our conduct, and sometimes our lives, through behavior that could have been avoided regardless of what our feelings are.

While making these emendations of Schopenhauer's doctrine, I am nevertheless agreeing with his principal insight about ethical life. Like him, I see it as a derivative of the compassionate concern that people often experience, either spontaneously or because they cannot ignore the suffering of others. Schopenhauer introduced his speculations about metaphysical merging between the compassionate person and the recipient of his or her compassion because he thought that this could explain how an ethical response can even occur. But the problem arises for him because he, like Luther and the Protestant tradition that Schopenhauer loathed but never escaped entirely, assumes that all of nature is motivated by nothing but selfishness. Just as Christianity had to hypothesize another world, a domain in which purified spirit prevails, in order to explain the very possibility of compassion or any other kind of moral and religious love, so too does Schopenhauer invent a similar dualism. He imagines an extraphenomenal reality in which merging that is not observable among human beings in nature transcends their normal selfishness and thus reveals how compassion can exist.

These mandarin maneuvers are totally unnecessary. Once we discard the dualistic perspective in Schopenhauer, as in religions such as Christianity, we can accept at face value the fact that nature includes compassionate as well as selfish attitudes. At least among human beings, we are programmed to be capable of both. Our reality, which is to say the structure of our actual experience, is a function of each in dialectical interaction with the other. There is no problem about compassion any more than there is a problem about selfishness. They jointly appear in human nature, and neither is more ultimate. They are complementary forms of life as we know it.

Those who are willing to adopt this naturalistic view must nevertheless show how selfishness and compassion are related to each other. In effect, Schopenhauer reduces the latter to the former, since the merged condition that he considers fundamental in ethics constitutes the reality of the compassionate agent himself, and therefore explains why he should make his altruistic gesture for the sake of someone who seems to have a different identity. To this extent, Schopenhauer anticipates contemporary sociobiologists who try to account for altruism by treating it as a subtle device for preserving the gene pool one shares with the other person. I will return to their idea presently, but even here I can remark that a more viable theory, one that is simpler and closer to empirical data, would recognize that some individuals, on some occasions that we can specify, are compassionate and therefore altruistic not as a continuation of, but as a corrective to, the selfishness that might otherwise have motivated their conduct. Altruism is for them a state of greater self-fulfillment.

What is the nature of this gratifying attitude? If it is more than just anticipation that we and our genetic kin will somehow benefit from our act of compassion, the consummation we experience must be explained in terms of wholly different coordinates. Toward that end we begin by mentioning the rudimentary fact that animals live in societies and are generally gregarious. These characteristics would seem to be innate for most species on earth. To live in a society, however, one must acknowledge the presence of other members of that society, and one must realize that they are similar to oneself whether or not they are closely related genetically. Much of what eventuates as ethical and religious practice results from these consequences of the "herding instinct," as it used to be called. And if one lives in a herdlike group with other human beings, it is unpleasant to see the suffering of those we encounter regularly. Through empathy we identify with them, and through sympathy we feel for their discomfort. By erecting standards of behavior considered justifiable or forbidden as a matter of principle, we protect not only persons who would suffer in ways that we deem needless but also ourselves as the reluctant spectators of their suffering. In the chemistry of our moral imagination, this joint protectiveness becomes a positive good and a source of personal concern.

While conscience and the sense of ethical obligation may be

explained in this manner, compassionate love includes a further dimension. To the extent that compassion is sympathy in action, it is consummatory as the material expression of our social feelings. But since it takes someone else's suffering upon ourself, and in the process often transfers the burden of this sorrow to ourself, one may wonder how this can be either a consummatory good or the basis of ethical and religious concepts in general. Compassion, like the experience of a hero or a saint, is sometimes thought to be supererogatory, exceeding the mandates of ethics or religion. And that is true. But because it is supererogatory, compassion serves as a fulfillment of the optional but typically human need to improve, protect, and preserve life. In the context of that need, the compassionate attitude is an affective work of art created through imagination and idealization that are consummatory, as all accomplished creativity is.

Emanating from this complex of natural impulses, compassion demonstrates that in life there may exist at least a rudimentary love of life. Life loves itself, much as the Western tradition in religion asserts that God loves himself. Each animate being acts as if it wants to perpetuate its particular mode of existence, which normally leads it to destroy life in other creatures, or even its own life when it resolves some inner strife by committing suicide. But over and above this love of self, there may also be a love of life wherever it occurs and whether or not it is actively suffering. Delighting in someone's joyful experience may not seem to be an act of compassionate concern. Basking in the sunlight that has descended on this other person, are we not appropriating goodness to that extent rather than alleviating sorrows? Even so, there is always a sad and sometimes tragic background behind each occurrence of happiness or consummation. We know that the other's joy will not last forever, or for very long. If this realization goes beyond the limits of sympathetic identification and makes us willing to ward off any harm that can befall whatever good appears in life, it turns into compassion toward life itself.

❆

When I initially broached these issues in earlier segments of this trilogy, I sounded at times as if I thought the love of life is the same as the love of love in everything, and that in their identity they serve as a necessary condition for anyone to have what I called a "significant" life. But interwoven as they are, these concepts are different from each other. To begin with, if we love the love in some object, we do not necessarily love it as the particularity that it is. Our love might be directed toward the thing or person or ideal not as it occurs uniquely but only as a manifestation of what we really care about, whether it be the Good, or God, or love itself. In his pervasive Neoplatonism, that is the stance that Santayana took throughout his philosophizing. When he spoke of loving the love in everything, he meant loving the object insofar as it represents or symbolizes that ideal goodness which is love itself. Santayana did not believe that love, or what he later called "charity," is addressed to the adventitious and idiosyncratic being of an individual person, thing, or even ideal. As it exists in the actual world, he thought, an object of love might be eminently unlovable in itself.

On my view, this approach to love further reveals the inadequacy of Santayana's ontology. He neglects the possibility that harmony between nature and spirit can result from love that accepts a particular as it is in nature. This acceptance is a bestowal that creates value in some object that would be without it otherwise. Love for the love in that object must therefore comprise a bestowing of value upon its ability to appraise what is good and to create additional goodness through bestowals of its own. Things and ideals cannot do this, but persons can.

In most cases loving the love in everything will signify an acceptance of the fact that some chosen object is activated by self-love needed for it to survive. Since there can be no possibility of love on the part of inanimate entities, we love them for what they are and regardless of their inability to love anything themselves. Even in organisms that we call lower forms of life, their biological structures being very simple and therefore devoid of the aptitudes that we possess, it may seem odd to suggest that they undergo love of any sort. When an amoeba persistently encircles an object it seeks to digest, can this maneuver be called love for that object? Just in posing the question we use language that is so metaphoric it may well be considered inappropriate.

Paradigmatically, we can love the love in something only if it is perceived as a creature that is conscious and clearly capable of bestowing value or importance. Human beings are endowed with powers of bestowal as well as appraisal, which is also essential for love, by virtue of imaginative idealization directed toward themselves or other persons, or else toward things and ideals. Many animals can bestow and appraise value, in ways different from ours, coherent with their disparate access to imagination and idealization. But the ability to *love the love* in anything is distinctly and exclusively human.

The ideal of loving life itself, which means a great deal to many people, has a much broader scope. It is not geared to an individual attribute, the ability to love that some, if not all, creatures have. Wherever we draw the line that separates life from nonlife, everything on the side of the former can serve as a suitable object of love. If we are so disposed, we may possibly love amoebas, bestow value upon them beyond the appraisive value that we discover in them. As an affective disposition, this attitude is not entirely different from the love we may have toward fellow human beings.

Being comprehensive in this manner, the love of life would seem to be less abstract and more "natural" than loving the love in everything. Yet this indiscriminate desire to love life in its entirety is beset by problems. For instance, can we possibly love *all* types of life, those that are inimical to our existence as well as those that are not? And even among the latter, how can we have an interest in, or awareness of, life as it exists in beings that are completely foreign to ourselves? Knowing so very little about their inner life, can we really be said to love them as the particularities that they are? And since the line between life and nonlife is difficult to draw, inorganic matter having notable though ambiguous resemblances to the organic, why should we limit our love to life alone? Why not bestow a comparable value upon all existence? We thus return to something like Nietzsche's concept of amor fati.

The difficulties in this notion that I adduced in other books are still troublesome for me. Though I can easily understand that someone might love whatever components of the universe are experienced as supportive to the welfare of that person, I cannot imagine an authentic love so extensive as to include everything indiscriminately. Much of the cosmos is hostile to us, most of it has virtually no connection with anything that touches our lives, and all of it appears to spring from realities that we hardly comprehend and are unlikely to decipher at any time in the future. Loving the vague abstraction that we nominate as "Being" or "what there is" can only stretch our capacity for bestowing value to a point where it becomes all but vacuous in itself and possibly damaging to any love of persons, things, or ideals that we may also wish to experience.

Having said this, however, I can see that a critic might use related arguments against the love of life. Is that, one may ask, any less vague or abstract than love for the cosmos? Of course, life is only a part of reality, and yet so vast and so diversified as to make us wonder whether anyone can truly love it in itself. But why not? Although we are matter, as basically all of the universe is, we are aware of our materiality through our consciousness; and that is embedded in vital processes that constitute the state of animate being. It is this direct and intimate link that enables us to love life wherever it occurs and whether or not we can love the cosmos that is needed for it to exist.

I am not suggesting that the love of life will, or even should, matter very much to everyone. Nor do I believe that those who are most accomplished in this mode of loving will ever reach the absolute goal for which they strive. The ability to love the tumor that will presently bring about one's death, as well as its own, is an achievement that hardly anyone can expect to attain. Nevertheless, the desire to have a love of life may occur in us as an urgent, though imperfect and incompletable, necessity for many people. In trying to salvage a saving remnant from the concept of cosmic love, we can reinterpret it as a disposition that excludes nothing a priori, an attitude that permits everything to be a candidate for our love. The same may be said about the love of life, except that in this limited class of possible objects we are more likely to realize our longing for indiscriminate love. The saints and heroes whom we revere have a level of success in this direction that makes us all feel that the ideal of loving life is worth pursuing as much as possible.

Apart from the consummatory goodness that accompanies the exercise of this affective talent, the love of life can be justified as a way of adding meaning to one's own life. All love is a search for meaning, which it creates through bestowals and appraisals as they interact with one another. The growth of meaningfulness that may result will be *significant* to the extent that the lives of others are thereby enriched, rendered happier or more meaningful than they would have been. The love of life meets this test splendidly, though often at a sacrifice of self-regarding interests we also treasure. The love of life is significant in a manner that transcends the kind of meaning afforded by an ordinary love of things or persons, both of which are inevitably circumscribed, or by a love of less extensive ideals.

Since the magnitude and pervasiveness of suffering that exists in nature at any time are so great, the love of life both manifests and presupposes compassionate love. In its differential employment of moral imagination, the love of life acts to eliminate suffering in any life form whatsoever. The specific mandates of justice, conscience, and ethical righteousness can be derived from this alone.[3]

At the same time, a love of life will include something other than compassion. Life can be joyous as well as sorrowful, ecstatic as well as despondent, comic as well as tragic. In immersing itself in the misfortunes of some other creature, compassion seeks not only to eradicate them but also to render conditions amenable to eventual happiness and fulfillment. If one has a love of life, one recognizes the multiple values it can include throughout its trajectory. When all goes well with us and those we care about, we love life as if it were a gift of nature. Optimists in philosophy idealize this part of reality, just as pessimists like Schopenhauer idealize the dismal aspects. Neither view is acceptable in itself: each must accommodate the truthfulness of the other within a larger vision that harmonizes both.

The brighter elements of a love for life are obviously consummatory and therefore aesthetic. Seeing, and taking an interest in, the gratifications that other creatures experience is itself gratifying to most people on most occasions. The imagined possibility of life including greater happiness or joy is a source of supplemental happiness that can become joy when we contribute to this eventuality in others. Though we may often be prevented by our own sorrows from delighting in the consummations someone else has, nature adjusts for this disability by allowing us to partake of pleasures vicariously and through sympathetic identification. We thereby acquire the ability to make our lives significant.

❄

In being compassion as well as sympathy, and self-enjoyment as well as selfless rejoicing in life wherever it succeeds, the love of life is relevant to every other type of love. It may therefore be considered a religious substratum of them. It shows itself in interpersonal love, whether sacred or profane and whether involving benevolence, sexuality, or heightened friendship. The love of life underlies the love of ideals insofar as they all presuppose that life is worth the efforts they entail. We pursue their objectives as superlative goods that we wish to bestow upon life itself. We care about it much as any lover wants the person he or she loves to flourish endlessly, or as a loving mother desires only the best for her child.

The love of things is related to the love of life in a somewhat different way. Things are incapable of experiencing either suffering or enjoyment. We cannot feel compassion toward them, and if we delight in their excellence, it is only through a metaphoric ideal of beauty or strength that we have foisted on them. A piece of music or a pebble on the beach that we fall in love with is not the recipient of any benevolent concern on our part. We appropriate its plenitude; we do not commend its being what it is. If the love of life enters into our love of things, this occurs through our realization that life is itself an offspring of matter, and that without things our experience of life would be devoid of content and therefore nonexistent.

It is this special awareness that sets the love of things apart from any love of persons or of ideals. It nevertheless provides a useful clue to the role of imagination and idealization in disciplines such as science or mathematics. For in them the love of things reaches its finest and most enduring consummation.

It may appear strange to associate the practice of science and mathematics, or even engineering and medical research, with a love of life. Since I am analyzing this love in terms of sympathy and compassion, these professional pursuits might be thought to involve a different attitude, preoccupied as they are with principles or data that can neither suffer as living entities do nor experience anything like the pleasures of animate existence. Above all in mathematics, which operates at a level of abstraction beyond the concreteness of the ordinary world, there would seem to be no connection with the love of life. The certitudes that mathematicians seek, and often obtain through their deductive reasoning, pertain to rigidly formalistic patterns that are quite remote from the actualities of life, or of nature, even when they serve to clarify them.

If one studies the mathematical or scientific mind more closely, however, one discovers that curiosity about inert matter and the possible permutations of abstract relationships is only part of what intrigues it. Whether experimenting in a laboratory or speculating in solitude about laws of nature, the inspired physicist will often be driven by a need to find meanings in the cosmos that are able to solve the mysteries of our own condition as human animals whose consciousness and spiritual aspiration must evolve out of the physical being in everything. Since that orientation pervades the mentality of scientists, some of them at least, it may also include a love of truth as a governing ideal that intersects not only with a love of the things about which one wants to know the truth but also with a love of persons as fortuitous products of the realm of matter who are somehow more than it alone. We are not our bodies, and yet learning about our bodies and their physical properties as a scientist does can reveal what is unique in our personhood.

Schopenhauer thought of science as a path of salvation that helps to liberate us from nature, the will, by discovering the means by which it wreaks its domination over our destiny. He believed that salvation consists in achieving a sense of dignity that comes from proud defiance of the will, repudiating it in principle even though it can never be defeated in reality. He assumed that the dignity and the salvation that science provides would be accompanied by a cold indifference to the data it discloses. He also knew, however, that through science, in association with mathematics and technology, nature can be harnessed and redirected, and that this may ameliorate the human condition to some degree. But Schopenhauer detected an authentic concern about the suffering in life not in science but only in the morality of compassion, which he assigned to a totally different compartment of spiritual endeavor.

I am proposing a view that is more radical than Schopenhauer's. Like Nietzsche I wish to emphasize the importance of accepting nature instead of spurning it. And I see in intellectual activities such as science a major attempt, not always realized by the scientists themselves, to treat brute matter as if it were a dumb animal or retarded child with whom one wants to communicate but cannot except by extending an exploratory kind of love toward it. An investigator who has this attitude may proceed through acts of identification, as a being who also participates in nature, and through something like a tolerant acceptance of its more backward components. Since the material data are not really children or even alive for the most part, the scientific approach I am describing is compounded in that measure out of metaphoric ascriptions not wholly reducible to the facts the scientist uncovers. But without the faith and patient attitude that justify these metaphors, the scientist might never have felt a need to uncover anything.

This is not to say that one should minimize the role of intellect or abstract reasoning in science or any of its sister subjects. I do not deny that they can be analyzed or reconstructed by reference to their cognitive components alone, as many philosophers since Descartes have tried to do. Most of them assumed that the rationalist approach was firmly established, and completely vindicated, by the scientific revolution of the seventeenth century. Nevertheless, science frequently occurs in the affective context I have mentioned. Scientific thinking, whether or not it is explicitly metaphoric, arises from acts of imagination and idealization that define its technical interests. Rationality, whether pure or practical, is a tool within this enterprise but not the sole determinant.

One might reply that I am talking about the art of doing science, or mathematics or technology or whatever, rather than the principles that structure them in themselves. And it is true that I approach science and the other fields in terms of their aesthetic elements. But those are relevant not only to consummatory possibilities and moral or religious implications but also to the content of laws that are considered foundational in science. Many physicists have attested to the fact that their basic hypotheses are generally poetic rather than literal. Mathematicians talk of seeing beauty in the conceptual patterns they manipulate, and they usually recognize that their prevailing love of elegance in a theorem or a proof cannot be defended on rational grounds alone. G. H. Hardy goes as far as to say that all nontrivial mathematics "must be justified as art if it can be justified at all."[4]

Engineers also admit that their technology is often governed by a sense of aesthetic rightness that exceeds any rigorous formulae in which they have been schooled, or could have been. Technicians of every sort rely on what they perceive to be intuitive judgments. These intuitions reflect affective and aesthetic intimations without which they would find it hard to function. By means of them, professionals become artists in their individual science or technology, which then exist as meaningful domains within a life worth living.

Because they must have specialized training in order to excel as experts, some technicians forget how much their expertise depends on their imaginative capacities. It is a cliché among scientists that science cannot yield certainty, that empirical judgments about the world are only probabilistic. If this is true, as we may well believe, it is because scientific imagination knows it can always find possible counterinstances to defeat any proferred generalizations about the available data.

Even statistics is an artifact of imagination. Though mathematics does provide its own type of certain truth, this occurs within the formalistic framework that imagination has constructed as a mental playground immune from the gross intrusion of mere factuality. Imagination operates not only in the formulating of mathematical arguments to be proved but also in the choice of rules that define the form of mathematics one is thereby pursuing. In statistics and other kinds of useful mathematics, imagination is needed to reveal how formal principles can miraculously elucidate reality. In mathematics that is not useful, the exquisite abstractions display the power of imagination in one of its purest and most aesthetic varieties.

If artistic imagination and the love of life can have a role in even the most abstruse procedures of science and mathematics, that may give us a final insight into the possible harmony between nature and the values subsumed under spirit. To reach it, however, we must still explore some further questions about the love of life and the element of compassion in it. We need to know what there is in nature or reality that brings these unifying phenomena into being. Are they innately programmed in the human species, and if so, why are they so often absent from our ordinary experience?

I opposed Schopenhauer's reply to questions such as these because it entailed reliance upon notions of fundamental merging among living entities even though they seem to be separate in experience. For me that separateness, and the particularity that results from it, is an ultimate given unavoidable in all possible reasoning about life. But while denying that animate creatures can escape the individual reality that distinguishes them one from another, I also recognize the sense in which they all are members of life itself. The life that runs through them has a pervasive character despite the great diversity in it. I am not the same as you, or my dog, or the beast that was slaughtered so that we could eat it, and yet at a very deep level of my being I sense the life that belongs equally to us and issues into comparable types of feeling and behavior. It is not just a question of my knowing that we are all alive, that despite our genetic differences we jointly participate in this rare and fleeting reality. Also, and of more importance, I find myself *identifying* with my fellow participants.

For many people this may happen only on rare occasions; and for everyone, it occurs in a selective manner congruent with some local system of valuation. Within the hierarchy of values that we bestow upon the world, different things and different bits of life will matter idiosyncratically. This affects whatever compassion or love of life we may feel. I personally find it impossible to love amoebas. A spontaneous sense of kinship with them does not exist in me as it does with dogs I meet on my walks each day. I care about these fellow mammals, as I sometimes also care about suffering humanity in other regions of the globe. But I rarely think about the insects that live secretly in my garden, or even about neighbors down the street whom I have never met.

Though our powers of identification, and therefore of compassion and the love of life, are sporadic, the mere existence of these powers reveals how it is possible for us to have a sense of oneness with life itself. This capacity, I suggest, is a potentiality in all human beings, even if they do not recognize its actual occurrence. I believe that life has built into itself a residual concern about the preservation and improvement of life. This is obvious with respect to our own welfare, but a similar interest extends to any other creature we identify ourselves with, whether or not it is related to us genetically and whether or not it is a human being. Imaginative empathy is thus the source of whatever compassionate feelings we may have. It is the ultimate origin (though not the *basis*) of ethics and religion.

Having made this affirmation, I may now return to my critique of sociobiologists who try to explain altruistic modes of behavior by reference to data about gene survival. They ignore the value bestowed upon living entities with which one has no genetic linkage, and they introduce a reductivist conception of organisms viewed as gene machines. This idea is as counterintuitive as Schopenhauer's notion of vitalistic merging.

If we assume that compassion and the love of life derive from feelings of identification that are innate potentialities in a species such as ours, we have at hand a more commonsensical explanation. Statistics about the likelihood of altruistic behavior toward those who are close to us genetically can then be understood in terms of mere propinquity. If the love of life shows itself most frequently in relations with individuals who belong to the same gene pool, this happens because they are the ones we know most immediately, from an early age, in a great variety of human situations, and within a network of mutual dependencies both social and interpersonal. Having identified with that much of life which appears to us under these circumstances, we can progressively enlarge this attitude to include other people and other creatures different from ourselves that we encounter in later experience.

The range of this enlargement is not identical in all species. In some of them altruistic behavior may be attached to conditions that do manifest a correlation with genetic ties. That is worth knowing, and the scientific investigations are valuable as clues to how something like a love of life reveals itself differently in the various organisms. But such information need not be taken to weaken our belief that despite, and underlying, these statistical frequencies there lurks a primal impulse of life to cherish and preserve itself wherever the determinants of individual existence permit. And, in any event, human nature defeats the findings derived from organisms alien to it inasmuch as the altruism, compassion, and love that we experience manifest biological principles that differ, in part, from those of every other species.

Sketchy as they are, these reflections may help us to formulate some conclusions about ethics, religion, art, and the good life in general. All social values, and all communication among human beings, presuppose at least a modicum of felt identification between persons in contact with one another. When communication with a nonhuman animal is sufficiently effective, we experience that animal as a person. It becomes for us a person that has no language, as far as we can tell, and few of the major cortical powers distinctive of the human race, but still a person nonetheless. Our ability to identify with other modes of life compensates for our inability to fathom what their existence is really like.

Identification with, and love directed toward, creatures that resemble us to some degree in appearance or behavior is as natural as our selfish concern about our individual welfare. Mill ignored the importance of this fact because he failed to see that whatever sympathy we may have emanates from our pervasive and untutored tendency to identify with others who are like ourselves. Though not yet fully moral, that tendency provides the innate possibility for our social and ethical values.

These are largely artificial, as Mill insisted, since they are highly variable devices human beings impose upon the wilderness of self-serving desires that nature has ordained as a prior condition for survival. But the propensity to identify with others, like the need to communicate with them and to cultivate a gregarious lifestyle in their company, is an important part of what is natural to us. We live in accordance with nature by developing these elements of our being and learning how to harmonize them with our equally natural selfishness.

Empathy is the agency of this identification, but it is sympathy and compassion that actually create the harmonization of which I speak. Sympathy and compassion are gratifying to ourselves, and therefore aesthetically consummatory, for they enable us to unify the opposing vectors that nature has instilled in its usual chaotic manner. Discussing the question of whether man has instinctual drives like other animals, William James remarks in *The Principles of Psychology* that our species has more, not fewer, instincts than others. We have so many, he claims, and they are so much in conflict with one another, that hardly any of them can assert itself with the exclusive dominance that we find in other species. What James says seems right to me, and I think his suggestion can explain the inner discord that so often ravages our human nature. Through empathy, sympathy, and compassion, however, we are innately equipped to harmonize some of the contending forces, particularly those related to explicit selfishness and overt love of life.

By building upon the instinctive capacity to identify with other creatures, sympathy and compassion satisfy our normal but conflicting desires both to help them and to profit from their calamity. We benefit from sympathy by being able to express concern about someone who suffers as we might in a similar situation, and from compassion by doing what we hope that others will do for us if we should need them to. We respond as beings who are programmed to take action against anything in nature that is destructive to life. When the other person's suffering is lessened by our behavior, we feel the mastery and the suitability in our capacity to do what we have done.

Critics might reply that my theory does not account for the considerable number of people who get their aesthetic enjoyment not from sympathy or compassion but rather from sadism and a psychopathic disregard about what matters to someone else. Such persons do exist, and their conduct may issue from motives that are just as natural as the ones I have been describing. But these particular responses do not lend themselves to social improvement. Gregariousness and the need to live in society are poorly served by the lifestyles of sadists and psychopaths. Men and women of that sort are therefore ostracized as failures and human misfits. They have a hard time as children undergoing their individual development within the family group, and as adults they are considered criminal or disturbed. The moral codes that characterize most societies, and therefore become normative for the species as a whole, repudiate the part of nature these people represent. Interpersonal love, not hatred, is thereby idealized within the group, and sometimes beyond it. Because that social love is also natural and consummatory in itself, it sustains whatever sanctions are perpetuated through the law and through each person's conscience or sense of good and evil.

By means of this progression the aesthetic and affective values that originate from empathy, sympathy, and compassion become transmuted into fundamental principles of ethics and religion. Great institutions are constructed to enforce them and to assert their manifest objectivity. They are not objective in any a priori sense or as the epiphany of an ultimate reality apart from nature, but they reveal whatever it is in nature that some particular society has chosen as the method of creating its own destiny.

❊

Since everyone is born to one group or another, the humanitarian sentiments enter into the pursuit of happiness as well as meaning, and their presence in both enacts a harmonizing function. As art is the agency by which men and women have consummatory, therefore happy, experiences through imagination and idealization that provide meaning in life, so too is there a type of art—the art of living a good life—that satisfies both our selfish interests and our compassionate feelings, uniting them to their mutual advantage.

In this grand aesthetic synthesis, we achieve the harmony of nature and spirit. All the values that religion and the religious attitude can properly accept enter into this synthesis, and all these values derive from one or another facet of nature. They all have a place in it. A good life, as I see it, includes the love of persons, things, and ideals so intricately intermeshed that the meaningfulness in each becomes a source of meaning for the other two. The totality eventuates in its own kind of happiness.

As a prerequisite for any such harmony, there must be faith of various kinds: faith in oneself, faith in other persons, faith in the material and social environment, faith in whatever ideals direct us toward life, and faith in nature as the only sustenance we can truly know. Faith is always dangerous. It can never be certain epistemically, and it may readily grasp at unrealistic, even delusory possibilities. But although it is not itself verifiable, except in being something that often gives us what we want, faith of one type or another is essential for human beings to experience love, meaning, or happiness, and above all a unification among these three.

In an earlier chapter I suggested that an immortality one might hope for is one in which we develop creatively forever. Death has no sting if it eliminates a life that affords hardly any goodness to oneself or others, a life that has shot its bolt and will never be transformed into a condition that yields novel consummation through further, albeit unforeseeable, imagination and idealization. In thereby suggesting what would constitute a good life that we might all want to have without its ever ending, I intimated but did not spell out the pluralist caveats that should also be introduced into the analysis. Despite the glossy appeal of this delightful dream, it must always be qualified by the realization that life is incapable of progressing in so simplistic a manner.

To see this, we must remember that much of the goodness we experience at any time comes from the loss of what we once loved and wanted to retain. Having been deprived of interests and of talents that mattered greatly to us, having suffered their deterioration or discovered how shallow their fulfillment really was, having been deceived or devastated by those who helped to bring them into existence, or having merely outlived these capabilities, we have to make a choice. Either we give up on this much of life or we somehow try to salvage what remains. If we do the latter and manage with some success, we may find before us a cluster of satisfying values that might not have existed previously. But the older ones will be gone forever. There is no way of restoring those cherished goods of the past, since it was only in response to their loss that we could have acquired the possibilities present to us now. Progressing creatively does not include the ability to perpetuate everything desirable that we may once have had in life. Reality is cruel in that regard, and would be even if we never died.

One might say that the goodness we gain in life is not always the product of a prior loss. And yet all of life can be seen as a succession of inevitable losses. Moving from childhood to maturity, we may experience creative growth in our personal development. But however happy and meaningful that may be, it also involves major losses—the loss of innocence, of inexperience, of unformed energy establishing its own boundaries. No one can develop in all directions simultaneously, and what one chooses to exclude at any stage is usually irretrievable. For everything we get in life, we must pay a price.

Once we attain what seems to us a life worth living, we may be willing and eager to pay the cost of preserving this goodness that we care about. But those who think they can have it free, for nothing they sacrifice emotionally and in their behavior, are deluding themselves. We would not, could not, achieve a good life without the beneficence of nature. That, however, is a necessary, not sufficient, condition. The actual attaining of love, meaning, and happiness, as well as their harmonization, depends upon ourselves, which is to say, our courageous commitment to the vital expenditures demanded by reality.

This emphasis upon the concrete circumstances in which we live is essential for understanding the nature of meaning, happiness, or the good life itself. The dynamics of our existence must always operate in terms of givens that define our individual space and time. In the course of human experience we move from the facticity of an earlier state to the facticity of whatever we have become in developing out of it. Abstract possibilities of happiness or meaning or what we suppose a good life would be are not themselves meaningful except in relation to opportunities created by the fortuitous realities of our birth, our innate capacity, our society, and the general environment in which these exist.

The diremption between meaning and happiness arises from the fact that a meaningful life involves ongoing and somewhat integral processes, as in the continuum of ends and means, whereas happiness is basically episodic. Though it may exist for months or years, happiness is a class of more or less felicitous moments. Even the happiest person is not happy all day and night or while asleep. However constantly they recur, the successive occasions of happiness can never make an unbroken chain. They are not unitary in the way that a meaningful pursuit is, even when its being meaningful makes us happy as a result of that meaningfulness.

If happiness occurs often enough, we refer to the conglomeration of happy episodes as "a happy life." A life that is also meaningful is made up of interwoven processes, each of them a continuum that is structured within itself though not uniformly, all of them changing and developing as life goes on. Combining meaning and happiness, the art of living well, the living of life as a work of art, transforms the overall experience of life into a totality that maximizes the frequency, duration, depth, and fertile consequences of the happy episodes while also assuring that the ones that lead to continued meaningfulness are given preference over those that fail to do so, whether or not the excluded ones are more intense or more seductive.

In various places Dr. Johnson laments "the hunger of imagination" that forces people to fill their hours with meaningless activities that increase, not diminish, their unhappiness.[5] When imagination is healthy, it does not operate in that fashion. Instead it enlivens life and makes it incandescent. Having risen out of the natural, like Venus in Botticelli's painting, spirit then fulfills nature and thus renders itself harmonious with it.

Notes

PREFACE

1. Ludwig Wittgenstein, *On Certainty*, ed. G. E. M. Anscombe and G. H. von Wright, trans. Denis Paul and G. E. M. Anscombe (Oxford: Basil Blackwell, 1969), pp. 15–17, 32–34, 81. See also Milton K. Munitz, *Does Life Have a Meaning?* (Buffalo: Prometheus Books, 1993), pp. 30–33.

INTRODUCTION: NATURE & SPIRIT

1. Isaiah Berlin, "The Hedgehog and the Fox," in his *Russian Thinkers*, ed. Henry Hardy and Aileen Kelly (New York: Viking, 1978), pp. 22–81.

2. *Inferno*, 5:102. My translation.

3. John Dewey, *A Common Faith*, in *John Dewey: The Later Works, 1925–1953*, ed. Jo Ann Boydston (Carbondale: Southern Illinois University Press, 1981–1991), 9:4.

4. Ibid., 9:20.

5. Ibid., 9:18.

6. Ibid., 9:20.

7. George Santayana, *The Last Puritan: A Memoir in the Form of a Novel*, ed. William G. Holzberger and Herman J. Saatkamp Jr. (Cambridge: MIT Press, 1994), p. 14.

CHAPTER 1: SCHOPENHAUER'S PENDULUM: IS HAPPINESS POSSIBLE?

1. Ludwig Wittgenstein, *Notebooks, 1914–1916*, 2d ed., ed. G. H. von Wright and G. E. M. Anscombe, trans. G. E. M. Anscombe (Chicago: University of Chicago Press, 1979), p. 73e.

2. Arthur Schopenhauer, *The World as Will and Representation*, trans. E. F. J. Payne (New York: Dover, 1966), 1:312. In this work, see also 1:57–59 and 1:311–26.

3. Oswald Hanfling, *The Quest for Meaning* (Oxford: Basil Blackwell, 1987), p. 5.

4. Georg Simmel, *Schopenhauer and Nietzsche*, trans. Helmut Loiskandl, Deena Weinstein, and Michael Weinstein (Amherst: University of Massachusetts Press, 1986), p. 56.

5. Ibid., p. 57.

6. Ibid., pp. 58–59.

7. Schopenhauer, *The World as Will and Representation*, 1:315.

8. Ibid., 1:314.

9. Ibid.

10. Marcel Proust, *A la recherche du temps perdu*, ed. Pierre Clarac and André Ferré (Paris: Gallimard, 1954), 1:438.

11. For further discussion of Schopenhauer's philosophy, see my book *The Nature of Love: Courtly and Romantic* (Chicago: University of Chicago Press, 1987), pp. 443–68, particularly p. 460.

CHAPTER 2: BEYOND THE SUFFERING IN LIFE

1. Anton Chekhov, "Ward No. 6," in *Seven Short Novels*, trans. Barbara Makanowitzky (New York: Norton, 1971), p. 120. See also Hanfling, *Quest for Meaning*, pp. 1–14.

2. Konrad Lorenz, *Civilized Man's Eight Deadly Sins*, trans. Marjorie Kerr Wilson (New York: Harcourt Brace Jovanovich, 1974), p. 37.

3. Ibid., p. 42.

4. For related ideas, see Gilbert Ryle, "Pleasure," in his *Dilemmas* (Cambridge: Cambridge University Press, 1960), pp. 54–67.

5. Bertrand Russell, *The Conquest of Happiness* (London: George Allen & Unwin, 1930), pp. 76–77.

CHAPTER 3: THE NATURE & CONTENT OF HAPPINESS

1. On this and other issues in this chapter, see Elizabeth Telfer, *Happiness* (New York: St. Martin's Press, 1980). See also Julia Annas, *The Morality of Happiness* (New York: Oxford University Press, 1993); Richard Kraut, "Two Conceptions of Happiness," *Philosophical Review* 88, no. 2 (1979): 167–97; and Marvin Kohl, "Meaning of Life and Happiness: A Preliminary Outline," *Dialectics and Humanism* 4 (1981): 39–43. See also Alain, *Alain on Happiness*, trans. Robert D. and Jane E. Cottrell (New York: Frederick Ungar, 1973), pp. 240–52; and Mihaly Csikszentmihalyi, *Flow: The Psychology of Optimal Experience* (New York: Harper & Row, 1990), pp. 1–22 and passim.

2. See Robert Nozick, *Anarchy, State, and Utopia* (New York: Basic Books, 1974), pp. 42–45.

CHAPTER 4: PLAY & MERE EXISTENCE

1. Moritz Schlick, "On the Meaning of Life," in *Life and Meaning: A Reader*, ed. Oswald Hanfling (Oxford: Basil Blackwell, 1987), p. 62.

2. Ibid., p. 67.

3. Ibid., p. 69.

4. See Thomas Nagel, "Death," in his *Mortal Questions* (Cambridge: Cambridge University Press, 1979), p. 2; and Richard Wollheim, *The Thread of Life* (Cambridge: Harvard University Press, 1984), p. 267.

5. See my book *The Creation of Value* (Baltimore: Johns Hopkins University Press, 1996), pp. 137–39.

6. Bernard Williams, "The Makropulos Case: Reflections on the Tedium of Immortality," in his *Problems of the Self: Philosophical Papers, 1956–1972* (Cambridge: Cambridge University Press, 1973), p. 89.

7. Lorenz, *Civilized Man's Eight Deadly Sins*, p. 39.

8. Russell, *Conquest of Happiness*, p. 30.

9. Ibid., p. 29.

10. See Anthony Kenny, "Happiness," in *Moral Concepts*, ed. Joel Feinberg (London: Oxford University Press, 1969), p. 45. See also Marvin Kohl, "Russell's Happiness Paradox," *Russell* 7, no. 1 (1987): 86–88, and his "Skepticism and Happiness," *Free Inquiry* (Summer 1990): 40–42.

11. Bertrand Russell, "What is Happiness?" quoted in Marvin Kohl, "Russell and the Attainability of Happiness," *International Studies in Philosophy* 16, no. 3 (1984): 21. Italics deleted. Russell's view is less extreme in "The Road to Happiness," in his *Portraits from Memory and Other Essays* (New York: Simon and Schuster, 1963), pp. 215–20.

12. See John Wisdom, "What Is There in Horse Racing?" in Hanfling, *Life and Meaning*, p. 74.

13. Russell, *Conquest of Happiness*, pp. 242–43.

14. Quoted in Alan Wood, *Bertrand Russell: The Passionate Sceptic* (London: George Allen & Unwin, 1957), p. 237.

15. Bertrand Russell, "What I Believe," in *Why I Am Not a Christian and Other Essays on Religion and Related Subjects*, ed. Paul Edwards (New York: Simon and Schuster, 1957), p. 56.

CHAPTER 5: LIVING IN NATURE

1. John Stuart Mill, "Nature," in his *Three Essays on Religion*, in *John Stuart Mill: Essays on Ethics, Religion, and Society*, ed. J. M. Robson (Toronto: University of Toronto Press, 1969), p. 381.

2. Ibid., p. 397.

3. Ibid., p. 393.

4. John Stuart Mill, *Utilitarianism*, in *John Stuart Mill: Essays on Ethics, Religion, and Society*, p. 231.

5. Ibid.

6. Ibid., p. 232.

7. Ibid.

8. Ibid., p. 233.

9. Ibid., p. 211.

10. Ibid.

11. Ibid., p. 212.

CHAPTER 6: IMAGINATION & IDEALIZATION

1. On this, as well as other issues in this chapter, see Mary Warnock, *Imagination* (Berkeley: University of California Press, 1976). See also Rudolph A. Makkreel, *Imagination and Interpretation in Kant: The Hermeneutic Import of the Critique of Judgment* (Chicago: University of Chicago Press, 1990), and Roger Scruton, "Imagination," in *A Companion to Aesthetics*, ed. David E. Cooper (Oxford: Basil Blackwell, 1992), pp. 212–17.

2. Theseus in *A Midsummer Night's Dream*, Act V, scene 1.

3. *Henry V*, Act V, scene 2.

4. Sonnet 29.

CHAPTER 7: HARMONIZATION THROUGH ART

1. *The Letters of Mozart and His Family*, trans. and ed. Emily Anderson (New York: Charles Scribner's Sons, 1953), 2:769.

2. See Irving Singer, *Mozart and Beethoven: The Concept of Love in Their Operas* (Baltimore: Johns Hopkins University Press, 1977), p. 6.

3. Archibald MacLeish, "Ars Poetica," in his *Collected Poems: 1917–1982* (Boston: Houghton Mifflin, 1985), pp. 106–7.

4. On this, see Jean-Paul Sartre, *The Psychology of Imagination* (New York: Citadel, 1991), pp. 34–40. See also Warnock, *Imagination*, pp. 169–71.

CHAPTER 8: ART & SPIRITUALITY

1. John Dewey, *Art as Experience*, in *John Dewey: The Later Works, 1925–1953*, 10:42. On Dewey's aesthetics, see Thomas M. Alexander, *John Dewey's Theory of Art, Experience, and Nature: The Horizons of Feeling* (Albany: State University of New York Press, 1987), pp. 183–267.

2. *John Dewey: The Later Works, 1925–1953*, 10:329.

CHAPTER 9: THE CONTINUUM OF ENDS & MEANS

1. John Dewey, *Theory of Valuation*, in *John Dewey: The Later Works, 1925–1953*, 13:229.

2. Quoted in John Dewey, *Experience and Nature*, in *John Dewey: The Later Works, 1925–1953*, 1:277. See also J. E. Tiles, *Dewey* (London: Routledge, 1988), p. 192.

3. David Hume, *Enquiries Concerning Human Understanding and the Principles of Morals*, ed. L. A. Selby-Bigge (Oxford: Clarendon, 1975), p. 293. See also Hanfling, *Quest for Meaning*, pp. 18–19.

4. I have argued to this effect in my unpublished thesis "John Dewey's Theory of Value: A Critical Analysis" (Harvard Archives, Harvard University, 1948).

5. *John Dewey: The Later Works, 1925–1953*, 13:220.

6. John Dewey, *Lectures on Ethics, 1900–1901*, ed. Donald F. Koch (Carbondale: Southern Illinois University Press, 1991), p. 37.

7. *John Dewey: The Later Works, 1925–1953*, 10:201.

8. Ibid.

9. Ibid., 13:202.

10. Ibid.

CHAPTER 10: AESTHETIC FOUNDATIONS OF ETHICS & RELIGION

1. For further discussion, see my introduction to Santayana, *The Last Puritan*, pp. xv–xli.

2. Act III, scene 1.

3. Percy Bysshe Shelley, "A Defence of Poetry," in *Shelley's Prose, or The Trumpet of a Prophecy*, ed. David Lee Clark (Albuquerque: University of New Mexico Press, 1954), p. 283.

CONCLUSION: LOVE, MEANING, HAPPINESS

1. Arthur Schopenhauer, *The Basis of Morality*, trans. Arthur Brodrick Bullock (London: Swan Sonnenschein, 1903), p. 275.

2. I am grateful to Ralph Acampora for this use of the word *symphysis*.

3. On this, see Robert C. Solomon, *A Passion for Justice: Emotions and the Origins of the Social Contract* (Reading, Mass.: Addison-Wesley, 1990), pp. 225–35 and passim. See also Lawrence A. Blum, *Friendship, Altruism, and Morality* (London: Routledge & Kegan Paul, 1980), pp. 1–42.

4. G. H. Hardy, *A Mathematician's Apology* (Cambridge: Cambridge University Press, 1967), p. 139. I am indebted to Rineke Verbrugge for having called this book to my attention.

5. On this, see Walter Jackson Bate, *The Achievement of Samuel Johnson* (New York: Oxford University Press, 1955), pp. 63–91.

Index

Library of Congress Cataloging-in-Publication Data

Singer, Irving.
  The harmony of nature and spirit / Irving Singer.
        p.   cm. — (Meaning in life ; v. 3)
  Includes bibliographical references and index.
  ISBN 0-8018-5426-1 (alk. paper)
    1. Life.   2. Meaning (Philosophy)   3. Philosophy
of nature.   4. Spirit.   I. Title.   II. Series: Singer,
Irving. Meaning in life ; v. 3.
B945.S6573H37   1996
128—dc20   96-16706